The Christian
Sexual Worldview

ALSO BY P. ANDREW SANDLIN

A *Comprehensive Faith: An International Festschrift for R. J. Rushdoony* (editor)

Keeping Our Sacred Trust: Biblical Authority, Creedal Orthodoxy, and Heresy (editor)

Infallibility and Interpretation (co-author)

The Full Gospel: A Biblical Vocabulary of Salvation

Totalism: God's Sovereign Claims in All of Life

New Flesh, New Earth: The Life-Changing Power of the Resurrection

Backbone of the Bible: Covenant in Contemporary Perspective (editor)

Un-Inventing the Church: Toward a Modest Ecclesiology

A Faith That Is Never Alone: A Response to Westminster Seminary California (editor)

The Birthday of the King: A Christmas Book

Dead Orthodoxy or Living Heresy?

Obedient Faith: A Festschrift for Norman Shepherd (co-editor)

Christian Culture: An Introduction

The Christian Sexual Worldview

God's Order in an Age of Sexual Chaos

P. Andrew Sandlin

Center for Cultural Leadership

Cover illustration, cover design and typesetting by Tim Gallant Creative / Publishing Buddy.
http://publishingbuddy.com

ISBN-13:   978-1517314798
ISBN-10:   1517314798

Center for Cultural Leadership
P. O. Box 100
Coulterville, California 95311
831-420-7230
www.christianculture.com

The Center for Cultural Leadership is a non-profit Christian educational foundation devoted to influencing Christians for effective cultural leadership—in church, the arts, education, business, technology, science, and other realms of contemporary culture.

To

Dr. Joseph Boot
God's man, my friend, and Canada's reformer

Contents

Endorsements

The modern impuritan American church desperately needs this book. The cultural crisis wrought by a runaway train of unnatural affections is now upon us. Andrew Sandlin's incisive analysis here not only provides us with a clear understanding of that crisis, but of a hopeful, practical, realistic solution as well.

> George Grant, Ph.D.
> *Pastor, Parish Presbyterian Church*
> *President, New College Franklin*
> *Franklin, Tennessee*

Acute and astringent, forthright and grim, this extended tract for the times calls Christians and churches to face the fact that the sexual disorder which America currently legitimates, radically and ruinously undermining marriage and family life, is a revolutionary tipping point in cultural apostasy, and to recant appropriately. Dr. Sandlin should be listened to; his case is, alas, compelling.

> James I. Packer, Ph.D., D.D.
> *Board of Governors Professor, Regent College*
> *Vancouver, British Columbia*

Friedrich Nietzsche argued that in order to properly understand a worldview it is necessary to ask of its proponents, "What morality do they aim at?" He understood that morality is frequently not the consequence of, but the driving force behind worldview formation. In this book, Dr. P. Andrew Sandlin has made the case that sexual ethics in particular plays a key role in this: "Our broad thinking about life doesn't just shape our view of human sexuality. Our view of human sexuality shapes the rest of our thinking."

The sexual revolution, beginning in the 1960s and continuing unabated (indeed, intensifying) to the present day, has been the impetus behind the sweeping changes in public opinion concerning some of the most important aspects of life: marriage and family, education, the role of government, healthcare, the practice of psychology, law and public policy, etc. The sexual revolution has shaken the cultural foundations of the West, leaving nothing untouched, including, as Sandlin observes, the sexual ethics of the church.

Incisive as it is concise, *The Christian Sexual Worldview: God's Order in an Age of Sexual Chaos* is equal parts diagnosis and prescription. Sandlin sounds the trumpet in no uncertain tones to the dangers of the "hookup culture" and calls the church to greater fidelity in holding forth God's truth concerning the divine intent and boundaries of sexual behavior.

Doug Enick
Pastor, Trinity Evangelical Church
Pratt, Kansas

My good friend Andrew Sandlin has written an excellent short book on the connection between sexual ethics and worldview. In his view, the modern sexual revolution is a central, not peripheral, element in the conflict between Christianity and secularism. His historical and biblical analysis provides a powerful incentive to oppose the current push, even among evangelicals, toward approving homosexuality and same-sex marriage. And his argument shows that opposing these movements will make a large contribution toward re-establishing the Christian worldview in society. I recommend this book to anyone who wants to understand this situation and to obey God's will in our time.

John M. Frame, Ph.D., D.D.
Professor of Systematic Theology and
Philosophy, Reformed Theological Seminary
Orlando, Florida

In 1996, Robert Bork authored a very telling book entitled *Slouching Towards Gomorrah*. In that volume, Bork both documented and lamented the moral decline that had already begun in the 1960s, with the so-called Sexual Revolution. In this book, P. Andrew Sandlin takes up the story and demonstrates that our civilization is not "slouching" but rather rushing headlong toward Gomorrah. In a word, contemporary culture has mastered the fine art of "defining deviancy down" (Daniel Patrick Moynihan).

The great strength of the work is its *biblical* approach to this dimension of ethics, as opposed to a socio-philosophical and consequently abstract methodology. From the vantage point of Scripture, Dr. Sandlin exposes the fallacious and destructive practices of illegitimate divorce, premarital sex, abortion, and homosexuality. Moreover, he takes to task the endorsement of these practices by various representatives of a putative evangelicalism. Insights include the observations that we live in a "God-rigged universe" and that homosexuality *itself* is God's judgment on a rebellious, idolatrous culture. In taking on "same-sex marriage," Sandlin reminds us that even Greco-Roman paganism, with all its forms of degradation, never conceived of such a relationship. In response, Christians should banish any thoughts of abandoning the cultural battlefield, but rather assume a prophetic stance of calling the world to repentance and submission to the kingship of Christ. These insights and appeals are all buttressed by historical surveys of the course of events that have brought us to this point in time, the "fruits of the sexual revolution."

All in all, this is a tract for the times that needs to be read, digested, and applied.

Don Garlington, Ph.D.

Independent New Testament theologian,
former professor, Toronto Baptist Seminary
and Tyndale Seminary

The Christian believer will find in these pages much needed wisdom and creative thinking to deal with the implosion of sexual ethics going on all around us in today's so-called "liberated" culture. Andrew Sandlin shows how sexuality is essential to the way one understands the whole of reality, otherwise called worldview, and how the Bible's teaching about sexuality is also an essential part of what the Bible teaches about the whole reality. It follows that getting your worldview right will produce a healthy view of sex.

Peter Jones, Ph.D.

President, TruthXchange
Escondido, California

This monograph cogently analyzes and integrates the three taboos of polite social chat: Religion, Politics, and Sex. Historically vibrant, intellectually keen, and robustly biblical, this work sets a new standard for understanding and applying the old, unchangeable sexual standard. By insisting, as God does, that sexual ethics is a subset of marital ethics, Sandlin unfolds a panoramically deep critique—and solution—for how we live—and ought to live—sexually, and what that means politically and religiously.

This work provides a turning point for this timely discussion, a discussion proposed not by religious conservatives, but imposed by the Left and its allies. All Christians should arm themselves with Sandlin's teaching here.

Jeffery J. Ventrella, J.D., Ph.D.
Senior Counsel, Senior Vice President of
Student Training & Development,
Alliance Defending Freedom
Phoenix, Arizona

Introduction

The moral bedrock on which Western civilization has stood for many centuries is crumbling. That crumbling, which parallels the gradual erosion of a Christian culture as the religious environment within which the moral foundation was first built, intensified during the 1960s both in North America and all over Western Europe. The result has been societies whose morality would have been unrecognizable as recent as 70 years ago:

> In virtually every Western society in the 1960's there was a moral revolution, an abandonment of its entire traditional ethic of self-restraint. All you need, sang the Beatles, is love. The Judeo-Christian moral code was jettisoned. In its place came: whatever works for you. The Ten Commandments were rewritten as the Ten Creative Suggestions. Or as Allan Bloom put it in "The Closing of the American Mind": "I am the Lord Your God: Relax!"[1]

At the heart of this moral revolution of the 1960s was the Sexual Revolution. This revolution, unlike the Marxist Revolution whose legacy the United States was fighting in Vietnam, has persisted. In fact, the Sexual Revolution has relentlessly worked out its own inner logic well into the 21st century, and it shows no signs of abating. This revolution is a part of a larger worldview. In 1982 Francis A. Schaeffer began his controversial *A Christian Manifesto* with these words:

> The basic problem of the Christians in this country in the last eighty years or so, in regard to society and in regard to government, is that they have seen things in bits and pieces instead of totals. They have very gradually become disturbed over permissiveness, pornography, the public schools, the breakdown of the family, and finally abortion. But they have not seen this as a totality—each thing being a part, a symptom of a much larger problem. They have failed to see that all of this has come about due to a shift in the world view—that is, through a fundamental change in the overall way people think and view the world and life as a whole. This shift has been away from a world view that was at least vaguely Christian in people's memory (even if they were not individually Christian) toward something completely different—toward a world view based upon the idea that the final reality is impersonal matter or energy shaped into its present form by impersonal chance.[2]

Over three decades later, it is certain that most Christians are less naïve. They understand that the rapid social changes in which they live are a part of a massive worldview shift. They understand that in some way legalized abortion and same-sex marriage and radical environmentalism and nationalized healthcare all relate to one another and all flower from the same stem. What they are less likely to understand is that the Sexual Revolution is at the root of that worldview and that, in fact, sex *is* in a distinct sense a worldview. Our broad thinking about life doesn't just shape our view of human sexuality. Our view of human sexuality shapes the rest of our thinking. Western society's sexual views and practices over the last few decades haven't changed so dramatically only because the prominent worldview of our society has changed; our society has changed because its sexual worldview has changed.

This book is about why and how that change came about, how injurious it has been to our culture, and what Christians can do to reverse it. I argue that (a) the Sexual Revolution is the most significant revolution in the West since the French Revolution and has poisoned every aspect of our culture (chapter 1); (b) in contrast, the Bible's sexual ethics have not changed either as they relate to the church (chapter 2) or to society (chapter 3); (c) sex as worldview shapes contemporary thinking and action in realms of life apparently far removed from sex (chapter 4); and (d) a distinctively Christian strategy for reversing this revolution and its worldview is a restoration of a full-orbed, biblical faith in every aspect of thought and life.

I delivered earlier versions of chapters 2 and 3 at the Westminster Chapel for the Ezra Institute for Contemporary Christianity in Toronto, Canada in July 2013. I am profoundly grateful to Dr. Joseph Boot, founder and president of EICC, for his kind invitation and hospitality. He is truly Canada's cultural reformer, and it is to him and his ministry that I dedicate this book. I am grateful to my colleague Dr. Brian G. Mattson for his helpful suggestions and to my friend Pastor Doug Enick for his eagle-eyed proofreading. I alone am responsible for this work.

Endnotes to Introduction

1   Jonathan Sacks, "Reversing the Decay of London Undone," *Wall Street Journal*, Saturday-Sunday, August 20–21, 2011, C3.

2   Francis A. Schaeffer, *A Christian Manifesto* (Westchester, IL: Crossway Books, 1982), 17–18.

Chapter 1

Two Revolutions and One Ethic

We children of Western civilization are the inheritors of two revolutions. Not one of us has escaped the effects of these revolutions. The first revolution was political and became social. The second was social and became political. The West of the last 50 years has arguably been shaped more by these two revolutions than any other two historical factors. To understand these revolutions is to understand our culture.

The first is the French Revolution.[1] This revolution set the standard for every subsequent political revolution. The Russian, Chinese, Cuban, Vietnamese, and Cambodian revolutions are only footnotes (even if massive ones) to the French Revolution. It was the first secular revolution in world history. The French Revolution overturned a corrupt and bloated *ancien régime* allied with a corrupt and bloated church. Like all revolutions that followed it, the abuses it engendered dwarfed the abuses it claimed to be abolishing. The cure was worse than the disease. Still, we can't imagine our world without the French Revolution. For one thing, it clearly established the state as a separate social institution, disentangling it from the medieval practice of allowing tasks we *now* limit to the nation-state to pervade all society—in short, the state gained a unique, separate status.[2] As a result of the French Revolution, the nation-state is a separate, discrete institution and recognized as such.

For another thing, the French Revolution ushered in an intentionally secular politics. The American War for Independence (whose
rationale was entirely different from that of the French Revolution)
did not formally recognize religion because the British colonies had
already established Christianity, and the new states all had an established religion.[3] By contrast, the French Revolution intended to
de-sacralize both the state and, by the state, the entire society—the
state as an instrument of de-sacralization. That is, one chief goal of the
state was to guarantee secularization. Only in the last few generations
has the United States followed the French Revolution and most of
Europe in this objective. Today, almost every Western nation-state,
and its society, is intentionally secular. This sociopolitical secularism
is the gift (that is to say, the curse) of the French Revolution.

The second revolution is more recent. It's the Sexual Revolution
(hereafter SR) of the 1960s centering in North America, England, and
France. It didn't set out initially to change politics. It set out to change
culture.[4] It viewed traditional Christian sexual ethics (the ethics that
had helped shape Western culture) as retrogressive and stifling and the
enemy of The Good Life. Its goal was to treat sex as individual recre-
ation, an end in itself. If sex is an end in itself, boundaries around sex
must be torn down as long as all participants consent to the sexual act.
Therefore, almost every form of adult consensual sex was normalized.
Mary Eberstadt proffers the best definition of the SR I've encountered:
"[T]he ongoing de-stigmatization of all varieties of nonmarital sexual
activity, accompanied by a sharp rise in such sexual activity, in diverse
societies around the world (most notably, in the most advanced)."[5]

The United States often refers to its War for Independence as "The
American Revolution." As Peter Jones suggests,[6] this moniker is a mis-
nomer. The most influential American Revolution in the United States
happened in the 1960s, not the 1770s. The War for Independence, by
contrast, changed politics, but it didn't alter society. The society of
the fledgling United States in 1785 was little different from what it

had been in 1765. Alternatively, the 1960s, and in particular, the SR, reshaped the entire social landscape: the expectations of men, the role of women, the planning of pregnancy in marriage, the fate of unborn children, the authority of the family, the prevalence of pornography, dating and courting rituals, and perceptions of (what were previously known as) sexual perversions. The quality and volume of social changes between 1965 and 1985 were dramatically greater than those between 1765 and 1785.[7] The 1960s were America's Revolution.

It's remarkable how the vast majority of controversial social issues today are the direct product of the SR: teen pregnancy, rampant divorce, abortion, parental notification laws, feminism, egg harvesting, artificial insemination, sperm donation, pornography, in vitro fertilization, homosexuality, and same-sex "marriage" (hereafter SSM). We simply can't imagine contemporary Western culture apart from the SR. Likely no other historical factor except perhaps the French Revolution has more shaped today's world than this one.

Fruits of the Sexual Revolution

Before considering whether the Bible's sexual ethics are outmoded, we should survey the fruits of this revolution that overthrew them.[8] While those fruits have included unprecedented sexual freedom, which many people deem a huge cultural advance, they have demonstrably produced such injurious cultural liabilities that the SR could never be objectively deemed an unmixed blessing.

Women

Ironically, the most injurious consequences have fallen on women and children. I say "ironically" because the fiercest advocates of the SR, social progressives, constantly profess care for the weakest and most vulnerable in our society. Yet, as with the case of abortion, their advocacy of the SR belies their concern. Women want a committed, loving man to care for them and their children. The SR often turns the man into a freewheeling, irresponsible playboy.

Women want men to do their fair share of the domestic duties, but the SR gives them no incentive to stay around the house—except to play video games, perhaps.

Women want romance, but the SR invites pornography that objectifies women and makes the female a Gnostic, unattainable, airbrushed digital photo that no actual woman in the world could live up to.

But porn has wreaked more havoc than objectification. Porn has degenerated into an utter degradation of women. In commenting on Gail Dines' "Pornland": How Porn Has Hijacked Our Sexuality, Kate Dailey writes for Newsweek:

> [T]he majority of pornography is now based either on women's humiliation (encouraging coeds to flash on Girls Gone Wild) or their degradation (the work of Max Hardcore, a pornographer now spending time in jail for obscenity), and the "women of porn world seem to enjoy having sex with men who express nothing but contempt and hatred for them, and often the greater the insults, the better orgasms for all involved. This is an uncomplicated world where women don't need equal pay, health care, day care, retirement plans ... It is a world filled with one dimensional women who are nothing more than collections of holes" (xxiv). And that world, now, Dines says, is everywhere: more rapes and sexual assaults, more feelings of inadequacy and shame, and less intimacy and equity among men and women.[9]

Eventually, sex is severed from intimacy and reduced to technique; in this narcissistic view, the aged and physically disabled are unworthy of sex.[10]

Women are the first great casualties of the SR.

Children

Children haven't fared better under the SR regime. Illegitimacy (but who even uses that word nowadays?) and divorce have wreaked havoc on children, leaving them often fatherless and splitting their time between two harried parents. Moreover, pedophilia and its gradual normalization have jeopardized vulnerable children.[11] This is not even to mention the most disastrous consequence of all — the murder of millions of children via legalized abortion, a horrifically bitter fruit of the SR. Recall that for the SR, abortion is contraception's "permanent backup plan,"[12] and it's simply impossible to envision the abortion holocaust without the SR.

Then, as they grow older and attend high school and college, the tragedy doesn't abate. Ours is a youth "hook-up" culture, meaning "one or another kind of sex act at any given time between people who may or may not know each other, with the understood proviso that the act leaves no strings attached."[13] *No Strings Attached*, in fact, is a movie title starring Natalie Portman and Ashton Kutcher about "hook-up" culture. Today's secular college campus is the Petri dish of the SR.[14] It's where young adults establish for life their sexual habits; and if those habits are shaped by the SR, they include sexual profligacy, male irresponsibility and machismo, and female objectification and abandonment. We also can mention date rape, egg harvesting, and alcoholism, the last linked increasingly on campus with indiscriminate sex. These are just some of the results of the great social experiment of the SR in the campus Petri dish.

A fascinating and harrowing effect of the SR on college-age women is how it pushes them to develop (irresponsible) attitudes conventionally attributed to college males.[15] The young men have traditionally refused to develop stable relationships with women since their first objective in college is to build a résumé for their post-college career: a sustained relationship would (they think) only slow them down in their quest of career success; marriage must come later. Therefore, college male-female relationships for men are about "hook-ups." Alternatively, as women have become more prevalent than men on campus, the demand for them has fallen, and, more importantly, as they have aspired to greater career success, they've shed any interest in stable relationships with men, which take time and emotion that they, quite frankly, don't have enough in excess to spend. In other words, they're acting like college men did just a few years ago.

This approach might create a terrific windfall if what women want is career success. It's a disaster if a stable relationship (culminating in marriage and a family and children) is what women really want — and are created for.

Men

Adult men would seem to have fared best under the SR regime. This, again, is ironic, because most social progressives are also feminists who deplore any male hierarchy; but if there ever was a male hierarchy in the contemporary world, the SR has helped produce it. Men get the freedom of recreational sex without commitment to a wife and children, and porn without social stigma. Men get all of the fun and none of the guilt — let the women and children suffer the consequences. This is the message, if far from the intended one, of the SR.

Yet men, too, suffer consequences. The irresponsibility spawned by the SR has bequeathed a generation of grown-up, effeminate juveniles who can't hold a job longer than a year, won't cultivate a woman's love, won't spend time rearing children, and know more about digital gaming than about moral character. They suffer biological consequences, too, and not merely occasional sexually transmitted diseases. Neuropsychiatry is showing that extensive exposure to pornography rewires our brain for sexual dissatisfaction: "Repetitive viewing of pornography resets neural pathways, creating the need for a type and level of stimulation not satiable in real life," writes Holly Finn in the *Wall Street Journal*. "The user is thrilled, then doomed."[16]

Porn isn't a harmless diversion; God is not mocked — even by a revolution as successful as the SR.

The Biblical Ethic

As heirs of this dramatically successful revolutionary *coup*, we Christians might ask ourselves: are Christian sexual ethics outdated? Since we seem to be losing the battle, should we abandon insistence on our ethical standards and redirect attention to (for example) gospel preaching (narrowly conceived) or uplifting life seminars or spiritual self-help techniques? The short answer is no. The long answer is: if Christian sexual ethics are outdated, then Christianity is outdated, because a distinctive ethic inheres in Christianity, and sexual ethics are an indispensable aspect of those ethics. More positively: Christian sexual ethics are presently operative because the Bible, the propositional revelation of Christianity in which those ethics are most comprehensively disclosed,[17] is presently operative.

This answer conventionally accepted by all Christians has come under increasing attack. No Christian worth his salt in the patristic, medieval, Reformation, or post- Reformation eras would have questioned the ethical imperatives of the Bible. The Bible is infallible, and so are its ethics. And that is that.[18] It stands to reason that the historical factors that eroded biblical authority in church and culture paved the way for the abandonment of Christian sexual ethics. These include, first, the 18th century Enlightenment, which did not deny God but came to deny his miraculous intervention in history (and what is the inspiration of the Bible if not a miracle?); second, the growing popularity in the 19th century of the historical-critical method, which reduced the Bible to the level of all other books; and, third, in the 20th century, the hegemony gained by the mechanistic-scientific worldview, which excluded from relevant truth any data that couldn't be empirically verified (obviously that means a lot of biblical truth, including revelational ethics). Not that the early opponents of biblical authority self-consciously attempted to throw overboard the Bible's teaching about sex. That tragedy was perhaps far from their intent. But once we cut loose from biblical moorings, we can never know where the wind of cultural trendiness may carry us.

One of the great anti-Christian thinkers of modernity who perceived where overthrowing the Bible must lead was Friedrich Nietzsche, who was well acquainted with the Enlightenment philosophers and took it upon himself as part of this own program to debunk their moral hypocrisy. It seems Nietzsche hated above all else two classes of people: (1) genteel 19th century Christians (his contemporaries) whose faith was not vigorous and masculine, and (2) 18th century philosophers who wanted to smuggle Christian morality into non-Christian philosophy. Nietzsche abominated this hypocrisy. The intellectually towering (though small-statured) Enlightenment figure Immanuel Kant wanted to get rid of the Christian God but preserve his morality so that society could run smoothly. Nietzsche would have none of this. "Have the courage of your convictions," Nietzsche was basically saying. "If you kill God, then you need to kill his morality too."[19] And Nietzsche did kill his morality — at least tried to. He countered with the morality of the "superman": man must invent his own morality. Morality isn't God-given; it's man-invented.[20] Fifty years before the SR, Western elites understood the significance of Nietzsche's message. The revised sexual ethics of modernity looked down on Christian sexual ethics as "bourgeois." The Cambridge Apostles, for example, an early 20th century cadre of atheist intellectuals, saw it as their mission to repudiate traditional morality.[21] It wasn't until the SR, however, that Western culture gave up wholesale on Christian sexual ethics.

What, specifically, are those ethics?

Endnotes to Chapter One

1   Christopher Dawson, *The Gods of Revolution* (London: Sidwick & Jackson, 1972).

2   Herman Dooyeweerd, *Roots of Western Culture* (Ancaster, ON, Canada: Paideia Press, 2012), 54.

3   Joseph H. Brady, *Confusion Twice Confounded* (South Orange, NJ: Seton Hall University Press, 1955).

4   Richard Wolin, *The Wind from the East* (Princeton and Oxford: Princeton University Press, 2010).

5   Mary Eberstadt, *Adam and Eve After the Pill* (San Francisco: Ignatius Press, 2012), 12.

6   Peter Jones, "Pagan Spirituality," http://truthxchange.com/articles/2008/05/06/pagan-spirituality/. Accessed June 7, 2013.

7   But on how the "conservative" culture of the 1950s laid the groundwork for the radical 1960s, see Thomas Frank, *The Conquest of Cool* (Chicago and London: University of Chicago Press, 1997).

8   For harrowing documentation of the next few paragraphs, see Eberstadt, *Adam and Eve*, 26–93.

9   Review at http://newsweek.com/pornland-how-porn-has-hijacked-our-sexuality-215368. Accessed February 17, 2014.

10 Kent Hughes, *Set Apart* (Wheaton, IL: Crossway, 2003), 79.

11 Wesley J. Smith, "Normalizing Pedophilia," http://nationalreview.com/human-exceptionalism/337010/normalizing-pedophilia. Accessed April 8, 2014.

12 Eberstadt, *Adam and Eve*, 36–93.

13 *Ibid.*, 82.

14 *Ibid.*, 92.

15 Kate Taylor, "Sex on Campus: She Can Play that Game, Too," http://nytimes.com/2013/07/14/fashion/sex-on-campus-she-can-play-that-game-too.html. Accessed July 24, 2013.

16 Holly Finn, "Online Pornography's Effects, and a New Way to Fight Them," http://online.wsj.com/article/ SB10001424127887323362800457

8456710204395042.html. Accessed June 5, 2013.

17 Specific sexual ethics are also disclosed in creation (Rom. 1:24–27).

18 Alan Richardson, "The Rise of Modern Biblical Scholarship and Recent
    Discussion of the Authority of the Bible," *The Cambridge History of the Bible*,
    S. L. Greenslade, ed. (Cambridge: University of Cambridge Press, 1976),
    3:298.

19 Friedrich Nietzsche, *Twilight of the Idols/The Antichrist* (London: Penguin,
    1990), 80–81.

20 Friedrich Nietzsche, *Beyond Good and Evil*, in *The Basic Writings of Nietzsche*,
    Walter Kaufmann, ed. (New York: Modern Library, 1968), 326.

21 Jerry Bowyer, "Perhaps Niall Ferguson Had a Point About Keynes,"
    http://forbes.com/sites/jerrybowyer/2013/05/12/perhaps-niall-ferguson-
    had-a-point-about-keynes/. Accessed July 31, 2013.

Chapter 2

Are Christian Sexual Ethics Outdated

in the Church?

On Ethics

The term *ethics* sounds cold and clinical—we get that sense in particular when we encounter ethical specializations: business ethics, medical ethics, environmental ethics, culinary ethics, educational ethics, and so on: "Dr. Snodgrass was fired after violating the faculty code of ethics by sexually harassing a graduate assistant." The word might be thought to connote the impersonal, as though ethics is a set of inflexible code that doesn't take into account human feelings or that, in fact, ethics was devised with as little consideration of human emotion as possible.

If so, this isn't *Christian* ethics. God—Father, Son and Spirit—is profoundly personal. Before creation God the Father was loving his Son and both were communing with the Spirit, and all three members created humanity in order to share that ecstatic, uninterrupted community (Jn. 17:11, 21, 23–24).[1] One goal of the gospel is to bring alienated sinners back into that community with the Trinity (1 Jn. 1: 1–3). Sin alone disrupts that communing. This is why sin cannot be identified merely as missing the mark; in addition, and perhaps more fundamentally, it is severing the communion between God and man. This definition of sin hits us right in Genesis 3, where we discover that the serpent slandered God's motive to Eve, trying to foment not just rebellion, but discontent, and we detect that discontent immediately, Adam and Eve sewing fig leaves to obscure their nakedness—they lost their pure openness with God. Their ethical misconduct was at root a relational rupture.

This is why sin isn't just a violation of a code, even God's holy law (1 Jn. 3:4), but also a shattering tragedy to God's heart. Anyone who encounters the Old Testament prophets and reads of God's grief (Is. 63:8–10), his weariness (Is. 43:20–22), and his fury (Jer. 21:4–5) at his apostate people Israel recognizes how profoundly sin fractures the loving, emotional communion between God and man. Sin is more than a violation of God's benevolent standards for man, but it is not *less*.

To rescind Christian sexual ethics is to rescind the Bible and its worldview (on worldviews, see chapter 4).[2] If one of our hermeneutical principles is that only the Bible itself can rescind its own specific teachings[3] (as, for instance, it does with respect to the old covenant sacrificial system), then the answer to the question "Are Christian sexual ethics obsolete?" is a resounding no—those ethics, which have never been rescinded, are not outmoded, and we must face head-on the incontestably clear biblical teaching[4] about sexual ethics. While legitimate questions surface about specific biblical ethics (like the mixing of seeds and fabric under the Mosaic legislation, notably laws designed merely to separate Jew from Gentile), the broad outline of biblical sexual ethics —what is sometimes referred to as "the moral law"—is bold, clear, and unvarying.

The Biblical Data of Christian Sexual Ethics in the Church

In broad outline, that teaching is this:
First, God created the sexes: two sexes, and only two, male and

female (Gen. 1:27). Both were created in God's image. Woman as the wife was fashioned from man's very body in order to be in the closest possible proximity to him physically, spiritually, emotionally and in every other way. Her chief calling is to assist him in their God-given task of stewardship-dominion over God's creation (Gen. 1:28b–29). While from creation she is subject to his loving, self-sacrificial authority, she is in no way ontologically inferior to him. She is not a lower order of creature but is equal to her husband in her being.[5]

Second, sexual intercourse is reserved exclusively for marriage (Heb. 13:4).[6] A big objective for marriage is the propagation of a godly human race (Gen. 1:28a; Mal. 2:15). The logic of God's sexual law seems clear: (1) God wants one man to be committed to one woman for one lifetime, and sexual intercourse as the most intimate act of marriage exhibits that commitment more than any other way except surrendering one's very life (Eph. 5:25, 28). Extramarital sex undermines the lifelong commitment of the one man to the one woman God has given him. (2) Since procreation is a primary objective of intercourse, God's ideal plan is for children to be reared for him in a stable family with a father and mother (Eph. 6:1–3). Extramarital sex produces extramarital children not formally tied to a single marriage and its loving nourishment. Christian sexual ethics starts with this law: all legitimate sex is marital sex.

Third, sexual intercourse is in no way sinful or even a concession to sin, but a delightful gift from God. The writer of Hebrews (13:4) states, "Let marriage be held in honor among all, and let the marriage bed [sexual intercourse] be undefiled, for God will judge the sexually immoral and adulterous." The book of Song of Solomon is a tender, sometimes erotic, love song between a man and woman as they prepare for marriage. There's not a trace of moral self-consciousness about marital sexual intercourse. It's true that the church fathers often had a diminished view of sex and the human body, but this was due to the influence of pagan Greco-Roman ideas. They didn't get this

conviction from the Bible, which depicts marital intercourse as beautiful, delightful, and holy.

Fourth, certain specific forms of sexual intercourse are especially
repellant. These include homosexuality (Lev. 18:23; 20:13), bestiality
(Lev. 20:15–16), and incest (Lev. 18:6f.). Homosexuality is repugnant
because it involves intercourse with creatures too much alike. Bestiality
is repellant because it involves intercourse with creatures too different.
Incest is offensive because, like homosexuality, it involves intercourse
with creatures too much alike.[7] The old covenant civil penalty for these
violations (like adultery [Lev. 20:20]) was death (Lev. 20:13). That's
how seriously God takes these violations of sexual ethics.

In confirming the ethics of the Old Testament community (Mt.
5:18–19), our Lord laid down broad ethical norms for sexuality in the
New Testament church. His teaching comes in two contexts.

The first is divorce. Jesus declares that divorce is not permissible
except on the ground of sexual immorality (*porneia*, Mt. 5:32; 19:9).
Adultery, of course, is a subset of sexual immorality in which at least
one of the participants is married. Jesus corrected false interpretations
of the Old Testament about divorce, but he confirmed its prohibition
of all sexual immorality.

In the second context, our Lord declares that it is the heart, not
the body, that spawns sins like "evil thoughts, murder, adultery, sexual
immorality, theft, false witness, [and] slander" (Mt. 15:19). We might
surmise that his point is to show that sin is ethical, not ontological.
Our problem is not our bodies or the external world as such, but our
sin, which resides deep in our heart.

In both cases, Jesus confirms the Old Testament standard that sex
is reserved for marriage.

The apostle Paul elaborates on this inherited revelation in speaking
particularly to the primitive churches. Two passages[8] are especially
pertinent.

In 1 Cor. 6:9–11 he writes:

Or do you not know that the unrighteous will not inherit the kingdom of God? Do not be deceived: neither the sexually immoral, nor idolaters, nor adulterers, nor men who practice homosexuality, nor thieves, nor the greedy, nor drunkards, nor revilers, nor swindlers will inherit the kingdom of God. And such were some of you. But you were washed, you were sanctified, you were justified in the name of the Lord Jesus Christ and by the Spirit of our God.

The second is Galatians 5:19–21:

Now the works of the flesh are evident: sexual immorality, impurity, sensuality, idolatry, sorcery, enmity, strife, jealousy, fits of anger, rivalries, dissensions, divisions, envy, drunkenness, orgies, and things like these. I warn you, as I warned you before, that those who do such things will not inherit the kingdom of God.

Both passages are striking in that Paul declares that specific, unrepentant sins exclude one from the kingdom of God. Those sins include (but are no means limited to) sexual immorality in general and impurity, sensuality, orgies, adultery, and homosexuality in particular.

Paul's point is quite clear: those whose lives are dominated by these sins (as well as specific non-sexual sins) have no part in Christ's kingdom.[9]

Note that Paul goes on to write, "And such were some of you. But you were washed, but you were sanctified, but you were justified in the name of the Lord Jesus and by the Spirit of our God" (1 Cor. 9:11), clearly suggesting that some of his Corinthian readers had been sexually immoral but had been washed of this (and other) sin and declared righteous on the basis of the atoning work of Jesus through the power of the Holy Spirit. His point is that the sexually immoral can, and should, be converted, but that in conversion, they leave their immoral (and their covetous and drunken) life behind.

Nor does Paul indicate that that these sins may never creep back into the believer's life. The apostle who wrote Romans 6–8 would hardly suggest that sin no longer has a place in the Christian's life at all, which demands a continual spiritual struggle. But it is a struggle that Christians are expected gradually to overcome in the Holy Spirit's power, and if one professes faith but drifts back into an unrepentant, sin-dominated life, he can expect nothing but spiritual death (Rom. 6:21; 8:6, 9, 13). Let me state Paul's reasoning starkly: if you live in unrepentant sexual immorality, you can't be a Christian. Your destiny is hell. The fact that this comment might sound jarring shows just how far the church has drifted from Christian sexual ethics.

In broad outline, Christian sexual ethics are abundantly clear. The problem isn't lack of clarity in the Bible; it's lack of fidelity in the church.

The Drift from Christian Sexual Ethics

The church, in fact, has not been immune from the Sexual Revolution (SR). Indeed, we might say that the church in general has increasingly been a nearly willing collaborator. At the very least, the church too often has been lazy and reluctant to insist on Christian sexual ethics. In this, as in much else, the church, even at times the evangelical church, has been accommodationist.[10]

The SR has reached its revolutionary agenda into the church, and the church has capitulated again and again—first with recreational contraception; then with easy, no-fault divorce; then with premarital sex; then (in some cases) with abortion; and now, more recently, with homosexuality and even same-sex marriage (SSM). This capitulation constitutes nothing less than betrayal of the sacred trust of sound biblical teaching, teaching which leads to the only sexuality that pleases God. This betrayal began in the pulpit. This isn't a new problem, of course; but the specific sphere of betrayal is new. And the fact that this sphere is the core of human life—marriage—discloses how dire our church situation is. The controversy over World Vision's stunning announcement in the spring of 2014 that it was altering its employment policy by now permitting SSM employees, and then its dramatic reversal two days later, testifies to both a residual backbone among even evangelicals as well as patent accommodation. Let's touch on several of these steps of worldly accommodation.

Recreational contraception

The Bible doesn't expressly forbid[11] contraception, even artificial contraception, so the traditional Roman Catholic view isn't (in my view) entirely correct. However, since the SR, artificial contraception has increasingly been employed to guarantee recreational, consequence-free, illegitimate sex—including for Christians. There's a fine line between contraception as a means of preventing pregnancy in a marriage whose wife requires a physical respite from childbearing (for example) and contraception as a means of eluding God's creational requirement in marriage to be fruitful and multiply, or a means of engaging in recreational sex for fornicators and adulterers. By her silence about recreational contraception, the church has collaborated with the SR.

Illegitimate divorce

Similarly, the Bible permits divorce on certain specific grounds, but the church has capitulated to the wholesale marital covenant-breaking (Mal. 2:14) endemic in our society. "Incompatibility," "irreconcilable differences," "boredom," "communication breakdowns," and "falling out of love" aren't valid warrants for divorce. The recent Western divorce culture is nourished in the historical outworking of human autonomy spawned by the Enlightenment in revolt against European Christian culture. It means: "I'm permitted to do whatever pleases me, as long as I don't harm anyone else." In time, the most sacred institution

God created, marriage, was compelled to bow before this relentless pursuit of autonomy. When the church refuses to hold its members to biblical marital standards, refuses to excommunicate recalcitrant divorcees, it collaborates with the apostasy of the SR. This is why the divorce rate in the evangelical church is similar to that of the surrounding culture. This is the price we pay for accommodating the SR.

Premarital sex

The church's accommodation extends to unmarried young adults. Two widely discussed recent surveys mentioned in *Christianity Today* noted that anywhere from 45% to 80% of unmarried professed evangelicals admitted to having sex within the last year.[12] The only controversy in the article was whether the actual figures are closer to 45% or to 80%. If the reality stands closer to the conservative side, this means that *half* of unmarried professed evangelicals have violated God's sexual standards. The pressing figure is one the article didn't address—how many of them *routinely* engage in illicit sex? How many are unrepentant, serial fornicators? Every day our sexually revolutionary culture bombards them with the benefits but not the liabilities of nonmarital intercourse, and the church often is insufficiently aggressive encountering this cultural bombardment. One reason they feel comfortable in the church, in my estimation, is that too few pulpits teach biblical ethics, and in too many congregations there's no expectation that teenagers and young adults will live chaste lives. The omission isn't simply negative—i.e., declarations of God's moral law; it's also a positive omission— churches don't spend enough time encouraging unmarried adults to be chaste and to exercise faith in the Holy Spirit to sustain them, and we don't pray with them and for them to live such God-honoring lives.

Delayed marriage

Moreover, too often we've purchased stock in the "delayed-marriage" ethic sweeping the West. According to this ethic, marriage is a reward for young adults already successful in their careers,[13] already financially secure, and already well practiced in sexual "relationships," having experimented with several "partners." This modernist ethic puts an onerous burden on young adults. The Bible, as I noted, recognizes the sexual drive itself as healthy; sex is holy and pure. The desire to get married and enjoy sexual intercourse and resultant children is a holy desire. Intentionally delaying that committed consummation in order to fulfill secular dreams of The Good Life is to defy God. Frederica Mathewes-Green is correct, therefore, when she writes, "Teen pregnancy is not the problem. Unwed teen pregnancy is the problem. It's childbearing outside marriage that causes all the trouble. Restore an environment that supports younger marriage, and you won't have to fight biology for a decade or more."[14] When the church accommodates the trendy "delayed-marriage" ethic, she subjects her unmarried adults to unwarranted pressure and reinforces the temptation to worldliness.

Abortion

Alternatively, and because of the efforts of Francis A. Schaeffer and Harold O. J. Brown in the 70s, the evangelical church's record in opposing abortion has been more praiseworthy.[15] Yet evidence exists that younger evangelicals are less committed to the pro-life position than their parents.[16]

Homosexuality

But the pressing issue today in the church, the latest transformation by which the SR is bulldozing everything in its path, is homosexuality. For 40 years evangelicals have capitulated to the SR, so why stop at homosexuality?

Rob Bell,[17] Brian McLaren,[18] and Jim Wallis,[19] not surprisingly, now support SSM; and in some cases, they're not entirely clear on whether they believe homosexuality itself is sinful. Long-time Fuller

Seminary New Testament professor Daniel Kirk (recently denied ten-
ure) recognizes the biblical prohibition of homosexuality, but publicly
expresses hope that just as God abolished circumcision as an essential
mark of covenant inclusion, so he might one day reverse his prohibition
of homosexuality (talk about a God in process!).[20]

The insurmountable tension in which all of them live is that since
they are often considered evangelicals they must pay at least formal lip
service to the Bible. But the Bible incontestably prohibits homosexuality
in the clearest terms; so these "liberal evangelicals" are increasingly
forced to jettison a high (that is, consistently evangelical) view of the
Bible.[21] They have come to terms (if only intuitively) with what one of
the early public mainline Protestant homosexuals, Gary Comstock,
wrote 20 years ago in his book *Gay Theology Without Apology*:

> I skirt established Christian Scripture and tradition to gain
> autonomy, to locate myself within my own life, to escape an
> external authority and find an internal authority.... This is an
> act of independence, not of rebellion....

> Although some of us [homosexuals in the church] have said
> that this passage [Leviticus 18 and 20, which impose the
> death penalty for homosexuality] is but a single reference
> in a huge document that otherwise ignores us, I have to ask:
> "How many times and in how many ways do we have to be
> told that we should be killed before we take it seriously. Is
> not once enough?"[22]

How many times indeed. Comstock is wrong; he *is* a rebel against
God, but he is honest about biblical teaching and doesn't profess an
evangelical bibliology and draw a salary and funds from evangelicals
while treacherously subverting biblical authority by overturning the
Bible's sexual ethics under the pressures of a trendy, apostate culture.

These biblical sexual ethics are no more outdated in the church than other biblical ethics are. In the matter of sexual standards, professed Christians too often practice "cafeteria ethics": they select those standards presently trendy in the wider society. Today that includes opposition to human trafficking, to ignoring the poor, and to racism. The Bible does support this opposition, but the fact that it just happens to align with trendy moral crusades suggests Christians who champion these causes célèbre aren't especially courageous, and when they neglect equally biblical ethics that are much less popular, these Christians are positively hypocritical. "Less popular" biblical ethics today include, in particular, sexual ethics.

In the prophetic words of the late Francis A. Schaeffer, "Accommodation leads to accommodation—which leads to accommodation."[23]

Liberalism 1.0

We usually identify this accommodation with theological liberalism, which, narrowly considered, is identified with a movement in Europe and America in the late 19th and early 20th centuries, but its theological impulse—to conform the Faith to the spirit of the age—has been around since the Garden of Eden. (In this sense, the ancient Jews, when they syncretized their faith with the surrounding pagan nations, were notorious liberals.) Liberalism's chief tenet is accommodating Christianity to the reigning spirit of the age.

In the first half of the 19th century in Europe, this reigning spirit was Romanticism,[24] the enthronement of emotion and feelings to counter the acidic effects of Enlightenment, which judged all things by universal human reason or objective human experience. The liberalism of that time did not want to give up the gains of the Enlightenment, but it also did not want to give up Christianity, as the Enlightenment seemed to be forcing people to do if they were to judge everything by universal human (as opposed to God's) standards. In this way, liberalism could protect Christianity from Enlightenment.[25] The problem is that the

SANDLIN | The Christian Sexual Worldview

Christianity it protected had nothing to do with the Christianity of the Bible. Christian beliefs—atonement, resurrection, Second Coming, biblical inspiration—are simply (in the original liberal view) a reflection on the internal Christian experience, which is the essence of religion. They are not true in any objective sense. Real religion is a particular kind of feeling. Whether the redemptive facts of the Bible are true is irrelevant.

Liberalism 2.0

Early in the 20th century, Enlightenment in the form of naturalistic science made a huge comeback from Romanticism (without negating the gains of the latter). Only what we can verify by our senses was worthy of belief. Anyway, science was granting society great new discoveries like Einsteinian relativism, quantum physics, atomic energy, and technology like the automobile, the airplane, labor-saving home devices, and so on. The miracles Christianity is built on had little obvious relevance to this science and technology, and they didn't fit into its worldview. Therefore, liberalism and its spirit of accommodation shifted from a religion of feeling to one of science. Liberals, keeping up with the times (again), questioned or abandoned God's direct creation of the world, Jesus' virgin birth and bodily resurrection, his Second Coming, and so on, so Christianity could be culturally acceptable.[26] It was this denial within the major Protestant denominations that spurred the reaction known as fundamentalism, which affirmed those very "fundamentals" that the liberals were denying. To be liberal was to deny the fundamentals of the Faith.

Liberalism 3.0

Today we live in different times still. This shift can be detected in the observation that while early 20th century liberal theological views were changing, their ethical views were not.[27] There was almost no dispute between liberals and fundamentalists at that time on what we today term ethics, particularly sexual ethics. In short, the liberals weren't parading for illicit sex or elective abortion or legalized porn any more than the fundamentalists were. This history of ethical unity and theological disunity is what caught many Bible-believing Christians off guard after the 60s SR infested the churches—including their own churches. Fundamentalism hadn't especially prepared them to address professed Christians who weren't interested in denying the "fundamentals of the Faith," but who were shedding the fundamentals of biblical ethics, especially sexual ethics. If theological orthodoxy is limited to affirmation of the fundamentals, then liberalism is free to warp biblical ethics. Bible-believing Christians were soon forced to come to terms with what theological liberalism looks like *in a sexually chaotic culture.*

It is now painfully clear, in fact, that the reigning spirit of our time is not naturalistic science, but libertarian sexual ethics. Just as 19th century romantic liberalism morphed into 20th century rationalist liberalism, so the latter has morphed into 21st century (un)ethical liberalism. Unlike orthodoxy, liberalism is unstable by its very nature, and its creed today is ethical (especially sexual) autonomy. David Mills writes:

> Unlike the modernists of old, our liberals are quite happy to let us believe in the Virgin Birth or the Bodily Resurrection, or for that matter praying in tongues, presumably on the assumption that it keeps us occupied and out of their way. They only object when we dare to argue for moral limitations and ideals they have long ago abandoned. They will tolerate the most extravagant supernaturalism, as long as it is not assumed that the supernatural makes binding statements about human sexual behavior.[28]

Not that today's liberals have recovered the great biblical redemptive truths. It's just that these truths aren't relevant anymore as orthodoxies to be rebelling against. Liberalism is all about rebellion against God, and its rebellion can't be limited to theology proper. God's latest great bastion that still exercised a degree of cultural hegemony in the 1960s was not theology but sexual ethics: "Aha, we've identified the latest, greatest oppressor to overthrow." The cultural milieu that today's liberalism must, therefore, accommodate is the SR.

This also means that we don't rightly identify liberals today by simply checking who won't affirm creedal orthodoxy—for the simple reason that creedal heterodoxy isn't the spirit of the age. The actual liberals are the Christians who are willing to throw overboard Christian sexual ethics—people like Rob Bell, Brian McLaren, Jim Wallis, and Daniel Kirk. By their adherence to the guiding spirit of liberalism—accommodation to the spirit of the age—they are no less liberal than were Friedrich Schleiermacher, Adolf von Harnack, and Rudolf Bultmann. And no less dangerous.

The discourse of sexual ethics

Accommodation in the church isn't limited to the 3.0 liberals; it also reshapes the way conservatives address the very issues fostered by the SR. The seduction from a vocal defense and practice of biblical ethics can be detected in the altered discourse of Christian sexual ethics among evangelicals.

In Christianity Today, Michael Le Roy, the new president of Calvin College, says:

> [H]omosexuality is a very real issue for [Christian] campuses. We have gay and lesbian students here. I have met with them. I have talked with them. They are Christians and they are trying to figure out, "What does this mean? How do I live?"

> The Scripture that I need to be obedient to leads me to the conclusion that marriage is a relationship between man and

woman, and sexuality is to be used in that context. I say that in the spirit of humility. It breaks my heart the way that statement makes other people feel. That's the struggle. I have said this to the Board of Trustees and I have said this to gay and lesbian students: We're going to continue to struggle with this issue.

Anybody who speaks in platitudes or thinks it's simple to be a faithful and wise Christian in these issues is overlooking something. I don't think there are very many people who report on these issues in ways that aren't clichés and stereotypes. The politicization scares me the most about this issue. It can throw a whole college off-track and hurt a bunch of students.[29]

We might inquire first, since Paul writes that unrepentant, practicing homosexuals can't inherit God's kingdom, how President Le Roy can call them Christians, if, indeed, he's speaking of unrepentant homosexual students, as he seems to be. Is he wiser than Paul?

In addition, to exhibit the full force of the altered standards of discourse on this issue, let's replace "homosexual" and "homosexuality" with "bestialist" and "bestiality":

We have *bestialist* students here. I have met with them. I have talked with them. They are Christians and they are trying to figure out, "What does this mean? How do I live?"....

Anybody who speaks in platitudes or thinks it's simple to be a faithful and wise Christian in these issues [of *bestiality*] is overlooking something. I don't think there are very many people who report on these issues in ways that aren't clichés and stereotypes. The politicization scares me the most about this issue. It can throw a whole college off-track and hurt a bunch of students.

Should students be "hurt" and a campus "politicized" if the administration opposes bestiality? Should hurt feelings be the primary objective in addressing a sin that God declares, like homosexuality, warrants death? Or is it a "cliché" or "stereotype" to employ biblical language? Biblically, homosexuality is no less repugnant than bestiality, and they are classified together in the Old Testament (Lev. 20:10–16).

Let's be clear: our heart should break for sinners (including professed Christians) trapped in this sin, as in any other sin. Their hope, and our hope, is the gospel of Jesus Christ, faith in our Lord and obedience to him under the Holy Spirit's power. No church should shun an unconverted homosexual open to the gospel or a Christian who has fallen into this sin and is looking to get help to stop it.

But why have some evangelicals adopted a discourse of non-confrontation toward unrepentant sinners and one of blunt censoriousness toward Christians who simply want to abide by biblical sexual ethics and use biblical language in evaluating this sin? The answer is accommodation. They're more interested in accommodating an apostate culture than in pleasing God.

We Christians won't get away with shining as light in a dark culture (Jn. 15:18–22): evil men and women will make us pay the price for following Jesus, including his sexual ethics. CNN reports that Christians who stand for Christian sexual ethics have become a "hated minority,"[30] sometimes accused of hate speech, with the hint that their speech might invite criminal action. For this reason and for the simple fact that Christians don't prefer to be labeled bigots, increasingly Christians who still oppose homosexuality are reluctant to say so. Joe Carter, editor for The Gospel Coalition and cited in the CNN article, states, "It's getting to the point . . . where churches are not going to say that any sexual activity is wrong."

This reluctance, too, is the fruit of evangelical accommodation.

Endnotes to Chapter 2

1   Michael Reeves, *The Good God* (Cromwell, Milton Keynes, England: Paternoster, 2012).

2   Vern Sheridan Poythress, *Inerrancy and Worldview* (Wheaton, IL: Crossway, 2012), 23–24.

3   Walter C. Kaiser, Jr, *The Uses of the Old Testament in the New* (Chicago: Moody, 1985), 197–220.

4   On the Bible as the source of Christian ethics, see John Murray, *Principles of Conduct* (Grand Rapids: Eerdmans, 1957), 11–26. The Bible, not nature, must be our guide. Natural law, like natural theology, but not to be confused with natural revelation, is a human construction, valuable though it may be: Herman Dooyeweerd, *In the Twilight of Western Thought* (Ancaster, ON, Canada: Paideia Press, 2012), 63. Natural revelation is a palpable fact (Ps. 19, Rom. 1), but the Bible does not invite us to fashion a theology to the exclusion of Jesus and the Bible (see Ac. 17:16–31). Just as systematic or biblical theology is a human reflection on the Bible, so natural theology (and its ethical subset, natural law) is a human reflection on nature. As such, it can never be finally authoritative.

5   "Sexual ethics" can include much more than the rights and wrongs of human sexual intercourse, but the expression has come to be limited to that sphere. This very limitation reflects the loss of a biblical approach to human sexuality, which includes marital, paternal, and maternal duties. The success of modern feminism, for example, should fall within the purview of sexual ethics.

     On the cultural impoverishment feminism has produced, see F. Carolyn Graglia, *Domestic Tranquility* (Dallas: Spence Publishing, 1998).

6   Sexual ethics are therefore a subset of marital ethics. The Bible offers no positive sexual ethics apart from marriage (for example, for single adults or homosexuals).

7   Robert Gagnon, "The Bible and Homosexual Practice: An Overview of Some Issues," http://orthodoxytoday.org/articles2/GagnonHomosexuality.php. Accessed June 3, 2013.

8   See also 1 Tim. 1:9–10.

9   Paul was attempting to acquaint new Gentile Christians with Old

Testament moral legislation that must govern all believers. See James B. De Young, *Homosexuality* (Grand Rapids: Kregel, 2000), 195–201.

10 Francis A. Schaeffer, *The Great Evangelical Disaster* (Westchester, IL: Crossway, 1984).

11 P. Andrew Sandlin, "Only God Gets to Define Sin," http://docsandlin. com/2013/12/06/only-god-gets-to-define-sin/. Accessed February 18, 2014.

12 Ted Olsen, "The Sex Lives of Unmarried Evangelicals," http://www. christianitytoday.com/ct/2013/may/sex-lives-of-unmarried-evangelicals. html. Accessed June 3, 2013.

13 Charles Murray, *Coming Apart* (New York: Crown Forum, 2012), 149–167.

14 Frederica Mathewes-Green, "Let's Have More Teen Pregnancy," http:// old.nationalreview.com/comment/comment-mathewes-green092002.asp. Accessed June 3, 2013.

15 Ed Kilgore, "Evangelicals and Abortion," http://blog.beliefnet.com/ progressiverevival/2008/08/evangelicals-and-abortion.html. Accessed June 4, 2013.

16 Anna North, "Are Young Evangelicals Sick of Sexual Politics?" http:// www.buzzfeed.com/annanorth/are-young-evangelicals-sick-of-sexual-politics. Accessed June 4, 2013.

17 Greg Carey, "Rob Bell Comes Out for Marriage Equality," http:// huffingtonpost.com/greg-carey/rob-bell-comes-gay-marriage_b_2898394. html. Accessed June 7, 2013.

18 Tony Jones, "Brian McLaren's View on Homosexuality," http://patheos. com/blogs/tonyjones/2012/10/08/brian-mclaren-clarifies-his-view-on-homosexuality/. Accessed June 7, 2013.

19 Melissa Steffan, "Jim Wallis Now Supports Same-Sex Marriage," http:// blog.christianitytoday.com/ctliveblog/archives/2013/04/jim-wallis-now-supports-same-sex-marriage.html. Accessed June 7, 2013.

20 J. R. Daniel Kirk, "Gay Conversations with God," http://www.jrdkirk. com/2012/04/10/gay-conversations-with-god/. Accessed June 7, 2013.

21 J. R. Daniel Kirk, for example, flatly denies biblical infallibility: "What, Exactly, Did God Breathe?" http://www.jrdkirk.com/2013/05/05/what-exactly-did-god-breathe/. Accessed June 7, 2013.

22 Gary Comstock, *Gay Theology Without Apology* (Cleveland, OH: Pilgrim Press, 1993), 108, 39.

23 Francis A. Schaeffer, *The Great Evangelical Disaster*, 146.

24 Isaiah Berlin, *The Roots of Romanticism* (Princeton: Princeton University Press, 1999).

25 Paul Tillich, *A History of Christian Thought* (New York: Simon and Schuster, 1967), 386–410.

26 Kirsopp Lake, *The Religion of Yesterday and To-Morrow* (Boston and New York: Houghton-Mifflin, 1925).

27 Harold O. J. Brown, "Evangelicals and Social Ethics," *Evangelical Affirmations*, Kenneth Kantzer and Carl F. H. Henry, eds. (Grand Rapids: Zondervan, 1990), 259.

28 David Mills, "The Bible Tells Me So: Everything You Need to Know About Morality & the Bible," in *Creed & Culture*, James M. Kushiner, ed. (Wilmington, DE: ISI Books, 2003), 140.

29 Katelyn Beaty, "Calvin College's New President Talks Budget Pressures, Diversity, and the Biggest Theological Issue Today," http://christianitytoday.com/ct/2013/may-web-only/calvin-colleges-new-president-defines-biggest-theological-i.html. Accessed June 4, 2013.

30 John Blake , "When Christians become a 'hated minority,'" http://religion.blogs.cnn.com/2013/05/05/when-christians-become-a-hated-minority/. Accessed June 4, 2013.

Chapter 3

Are Christian Sexual Ethics Outdated

in the Culture?

If Christian sexual ethics are authoritative in the church, there can be no question about their normative character: God desires and demands that his people obey him sexually in a particular way. But does this sexual normativity transcend the church? Does God demand exclusively marital heterosexuality, for example, of *everyone*? He does. It does not require a long chapter to prove this assertion.

The Biblical Data of Christian Sexual Ethics in the Culture

Both the Old and New Testaments teach that God's sexual ethics bind believer and unbeliever alike. While the so-called cultic or sacrificial stipulations of the old covenant were temporary (and were always meant to be temporary [Heb. 9:6–10]), sexual ethics are indispensable stipulations of the moral law that reflect God's unchanging character. Laws forbidding rape, incest, fornication, bestiality, adultery, and so forth are not laws designed to erect a temporary typical barrier between Jew and Gentile, nor temporary laws prefiguring the redemptive work of the coming Messiah, Jesus Christ. Rather, these sexual laws (part of what we might call God's *moral* law) depict God's immutable character and therefore can no more pass away than he can pass away. For this reason Jesus verifies the authority of the revelatory moral law (Mt. 5:17–18), and Paul trumpets: "[T]he law is holy, and the commandment is holy and righteous and good" (Rom. 7:12). Paul's quarrel was never with the moral law as such but only with the widespread attempt to abstract that law from Jesus Christ and turn it into a system of works-righteousness.[1]

We shouldn't be surprised, therefore, that in the Old Testament God's moral law binds Gentiles, not only Jews. He warns Israel that it was precisely for the Gentiles' violation of his moral law (that he delivered to the Jews as the Ten Commandments) that he expelled the pagans from Canaan (Dt. 8:11–20). God inspired the Jewish prophets to indict the pagan Gentiles for their depravity right alongside the Jews (Is. 14–24).[2]

The New Testament reinforces this theme. In Romans 1 Paul catalogs the sins of the Gentiles that incite his judgment. These sins are all violations of the Old Testament moral law (1:29–31). Paul goes on to indict the Jews for *these same sins* (2:1). He writes that the Gentiles, who lacked the written law, will be judged by their conscience, on which God has written that law (2:12, 15–16). The Jews, meanwhile, will be judged by the written Mosaic law, which God had graciously bestowed on them (2:12b, 17–29, 3:1–3). It's critical to note that Jew and Gentile are judged for violating the *same* moral law. This is why Paul goes on to declare (3:19): "Now we know that whatever the law says it speaks to those who are under the law, so that *every* mouth may be stopped, and the *whole world* may be held accountable to God." God's moral stipulations bind all humanity, not just the Jews or the church.[3] The cost of breaking God's moral law is steep, not just eternally in hell (Rom. 2:8–9), but temporally on earth (1:27; see also Gal. 6:7–8).

Same-sex "marriage"

I'll elaborate on homosexuality, since it's such a hot-button issue in our time, and despite the fact that, as *The Atlantic* puts it, "Americans

Have No Idea How Few Gay People There Are."[4] Homosexuality isn't new. It's likely nearly as old as human sexuality itself. Some societies have been rife with it, and not just ancient Sodom and Gomorrah. What *is* new is the public normalization and ultimate legal recognition of homosexuality—specifically, same-sex marriage (SSM), which is the pressing social issue of our time. It's not pressing because Christians have pressed it. It's pressing because homosexuals have relentlessly pressed for utter social routinization.[5] SSM is merely the latest step in their radical routinization agenda.

The very notion of SSM verifies the startling and swift success of the homosexual agenda, which has been to routinize homosexuality in modern culture.

By "routinization" I mean the blithe acceptance of homosexuality as no more odd than relatively rare human social phenomena like red-headedness or left-handedness. We wouldn't say redheaded or left-handed people shouldn't marry, would we? This is routinization. Its next agenda item, cultural routinization, is to marginalize and oppress anyone who either vocally opposes or, in time, refuses to support homosexuality.

Unqualified denunciation in the Bible

In light of this routinization program, including among prominent evangelicals, we might wish to revisit the Bible's teaching regarding it.[6] The notorious case of God's incineration of the cities of Sodom and Gomorrah (Gen. 19–20) is the first time we obviously encounter this sin. This episode is significant because it predates the divinely dictated moral law given at Sinai and, so far as we know, was not a part of God's propositional revelation orally communicated. It shows that homosexuality is such an obvious sin that it can be known in nature (Paul says this explicitly in the New Testament [Rom. 1:18–32]). Nature was created by God. We live in a God-rigged universe. This is why no one ever gets away with sin (Gal. 6:7–8). While sin is a personal affront to God, and while he punishes it personally, he also designed the universe itself as a disincentive to sin. One disincentive is that it discloses to our conscience specific grievous sins that we *know* (in spite of what we might *say* we know) deserve God's wrath. According to Paul, one of those sins is homosexuality (Rom. 1:29–32). So, the men of Sodom not only were sinful; they *knew* they were sinful and they knew their sin deserved God's wrath, just as homosexuals (and others) know in their heart of hearts today (Rom. 1:32).

God was grieved by the sin of these cities, and dispatched two angels (embodied as young men) to investigate further. When the men of the city heard that the angels had lodged with Lot, a godly man, they bombarded the house and demanded that Lot turn over the angels so that the men of Sodom might "know" them. That is a biblical euphemism for the intimacy of sexual intercourse (see Gen. 4:1; 1 Sam. 1:19; Jud. 19:25). Lot refused to turn the angels over to the mob, though he did (horrifically) offer them his daughters for their sexual pleasure. In the end, Lot and his family escaped Sodom (though his wife perished for her direct disobedience).

The Bible states that God incinerated these cites because of their unrepentant evil. There's no dispute about what the text says. There is equally no dispute about what specific sin incited God's wrath, at least, that is, not among people committed to the Bible as God's word. God hates homosexuality, and he incinerated two ancient cites that were enamored with it.

In Leviticus 18 and 20, God lays out his verdict on homosexuality in articulating the sexual regulations of his moral law to ancient Israel. That verdict is blunt:

You shall not lie with a male as with a woman; it is an abomination (18:22).

If a man lies with a male as with a woman, both of them have committed an abomination; they shall surely be put to death; their blood is upon them (20:13).

Both passages appear in lists of prohibited sexual behavior, including bestiality and incest. Both times the sin of homosexuality is described as an abomination. The Hebrew expression refers either to ritual or ethical uncleanness,[7] so it will not suffice to say, as some critics of the conventional view do, that the fact that certain foods are also deemed unclean in this passage shows that homosexuality was obviously a ritual (a temporary) uncleanness.[8] Homosexuality, like other sexual sins, is detestable in God's sight. In these passages it is homosexuality, and not the other violations, that demands the death penalty. The fact that the law prescribed this penalty even if both guilty parties are unmarried exhibits that the death penalty was not leveled on account of any adultery (this was not the case with simple heterosexual fornication). The rationale for this law was chiefly the prevention of the inversion of procreation, and Robert Adler observes: "[A]ny simulation of procreative heterosexual intercourse by the insertion of the male member in an orifice or fleshy crevice of another male is abhorrent."[9]

There is no serious dispute about the general import of this passage, no matter how individuals may wrangle over the particulars.

We've already surveyed Paul's teaching to the churches at Corinth and Galatia. But his most extensive and forceful treatment of homosexuality is found in Romans 1, which catalogs the sins of the Gentiles (in distinction from God's covenant people), exposing them to God's righteous anger. Paul mentions both male homosexuality (v. 27) as well as what we today term lesbianism (v. 26). He refers to this sin as "dishonoring their bodies [= treating their bodies with contempt] among themselves" (v. 24). It's "contrary to nature" (vv. 26–27), and like idolatry is a "deliberate suppression of the truth available to the pagans in the world around them."[10] This is why Paul links idolatry and homosexuality; both are intentional assaults on God's moral law disclosed in nature, not only in the Bible.

Two other chilling facts stand out. First, Paul doesn't say that God will judge homosexuality; he says that homosexuality *itself* is God's judgment on a rebellious, idolatrous culture (vv. 24–28). God handed the ancient pagans over to homosexuality since they had turned their back on him to worship and serve idols.[11] The consequences of homosexuality on the human body and life constitute God's temporal judgment (v. 27b). Eternal judgment comes later.

Second, we can infer that for Paul, homosexuality is the ultimate cultural sin.[12] In Romans 1, Paul teaches that because of the Gentiles' idolatry, God "turned them over" to homosexuality. As counterintuitive as this judgment may seem to our modern (in)sensibilities, it demonstrates that God views homosexuality as a self-destructive act (Rom. 1:26–28) that is a suitable punishment for apostasy.

We shouldn't be misled that every sin is equally repugnant to God and worthy of equal temporal judgment by statements like "whoever keeps the whole law but fails in one point has become accountable for all of it" (Jas. 2:10). Mark 3:29 (for example) refers to blasphemy against the Holy Spirit as an "eternal sin" that cannot be forgiven. Obviously this sin is weightier than others. Analogously, homosexuality as social depravity is the culmination of an apostate culture. When we detect wholesale homosexual practice, we are witnessing God's judgment on a culture.

We don't know how many homosexuals reside in North America:

The Williams Institute at the UCLA School of Law, a sexual orientation law and public policy think tank, estimates that 9 million (about 3.8%) of Americans identify as gay, lesbian, bisexual or transgender (2011). The institute also found that bisexuals make up 1.8% of the population, while 1.7% are gay or lesbian. Transgender adults make up 0.3% of the population.[13]

Whatever the accurate figures, homosexuals constitute a minute minority (as I noted in chapter 2), despite the perception (with a PR windfall for the homosexual agenda) that homosexuality is pervasive. Especially troubling is increasing approval and solemnization of this perversity as marriage. Perhaps in some sense it is this cultural approbation by heterosexuals that angers God even more than sexual perversion itself (see Rom. 1:18, 32).

This cultural homosexualization is not a stand-alone issue but simply the latest in an extended apostasy springing from an anti-biblical worldview. When a single controversial social issue like SSM (or abortion or government-mandated health care) pervades public discourse, Christians often assess it as non-Christians present it: a single issue that must be discussed, and accepted or rejected on its own merits. This is a fatal strategic error, because social issues such as these are simply single examples of a larger anti-Christian worldview. I'll turn next to explaining that worldview as it relates to sexual ethics.

Endnotes to Chapter 3

1   Daniel P. Fuller, *Gospel and Law* (Grand Rapids: Eerdmans, 1980).

2   Carl F. H. Henry, *God, Revelation and Authority* (Waco, TX: Word, 1983),
     6:442. No sector of the church has recognized this truth as clearly as the
     Reformed: "The Calvinist insists that the principles of God's Word are
     valid not only for himself but for all citizens. Since God is to be owned
     as Sovereign by everyone, whether he so wishes or not, so also the Bible
     should be the determining rule for all," H. Henry Meeter, *The Basic Ideas of
     Calvinism* (Grand Rapids: Kregel, 1960 edition), 99.

3   C. E. B. Cranfield, *Romans 1–8* (London and New York: T & T Clark,
     2001 edition), 196.

4   Garance Franke-Ruta, "Americans Have No Idea How Few Gay People
     There Are," http://www.theatlantic.com/politics/archive/2012/05/
     americans-have-no-idea-how-few-gay-people-there-are/257753/.
     Accessed August 13, 2014. Americans on average believe that about 25%
     of the nation is homosexual. The actual figure is lower than 4%.

5   Dennis Altman, *The Homosexualization of America* (Boston: Beacon, 1982).

6   For exhaustive exegetical documentation, see Robert A. J. Gagnon, *The
     Bible and Homosexual Practice* (Nashville, TN: Abington Press, 2001).

7   Robert Adler, *The Five Books of Moses* (New York and London: W. W.
     Norton, 2004), 624.

8   Greg L. Bahnsen, *Homosexuality* (Nacogdoches, TX: Covenant Media,
     2011), 31.

9   Robert Adler, *The Five Books of Moses*, 624.

10   Robert Gagnon, *The Bible and Homosexual Practice*, 254.

11   Brian G. Mattson, "The Judgment of Continuity," http://drbrianmattson.
     com/journal/2013/6/3/the-judgment-of-continuity. Accessed February
     18, 2014.

12   John E. Ashbrook, "Homosexuality: The Ultimate Sin, Part II," in *The
     Projector*, November-December, 1983, 6–7.

13   Ramon Johnson, "Gay Population Statistics: How Many Gay People
     Are There?" http://gaylife.about.com/od/comingout/a/population.htm.
     Accessed June 5, 2013.

Chapter 4

The Christian Sexual Worldview

In chapter 2, I outlined the Bible's basic teaching regarding human sexuality. In this chapter, I'm elaborating on that teaching by suggesting that sex is part of a Christian (i.e., biblical) worldview—and, for that matter, a part of everyone's worldview. A worldview is a way of viewing the world, and it's a big topic among Christianity these days. The word (at least its German equivalent) was first used by Enlightenment philosopher Immanuel Kant,[1] and it has come to mean, in James H. Olthius's words, "a framework or set of fundamental beliefs through which we view the world and our calling and future in it."[2] Because sex is at the root of humanity's God-given cultural mandate (Gen. 1:26–28), it's near the very center of a biblical worldview. This is also why people line up on different sides of a deep chasm between sexual issues that stand or fall as a unit: premarital sex, homosexuality, pornography, abortion, and birth control.[3] It's rare to find hardcore pro-abortionists who are anti-homosexual, for example, or people with lenient views of porn who oppose birth control. Sex is worldview.

The fact that so many Christians today can speak so frequently about worldview without considering sex is likely the result of their impoverished view of creation: if they recognized that a Christian sexual worldview (CSW) begins where the Bible does, in Genesis, with creation, and not in John 3:16, or in the book of Romans, with redemption, they'd not make that strategic omission.[4] In any case, sex is so central to God's plan for humanity and creation that we can't have a fully biblical understanding of sex itself without a CSW and how sex contributes to our—and everybody's—worldview. Just as important, I intend to show how worldview shapes specific sexual views and practices: consistent Christians maintain a consistently Christian approach to and practice of sex.

Sex in the Biblical Worldview

Sex and creation

First, since God created man as (sexual) male and woman as (sexual) female, sex is grounded in a creational, not a cultural, reality. John M. Frame captures this distinction: "Creation is what God makes; culture is what we make."[5] Culture, strictly defined, denotes those products of human interactivity with nature that reflect the self-conscious goal of human benefit: education, science, entertainment, technology, architecture, the arts—even such simple human products as meals, toys, and personal grooming products. The category of culture introduces a sharp divide from nature. We know that God created nature: it is his handiwork. God does not create culture—not directly anyway.

Culture is quite different from creation; its distinctive trait is the human use of that creation for man's benefit. Culture is what we get when man intentionally employs creation for beneficial purposes. A tomato is not an aspect of culture; a pizza is. Oxygen is not an example of culture; an oxygen mask is. King David is not defined as culture; Michelangelo's famous sculpture *King David* (c. 1504) is an example of culture. Creation plus man's beneficial interaction with it equals culture.

Culture is a human construction. Better: it is a human reconstruction[6] of the created world (material or immaterial) from the hand of God. Human sexuality is an example of creation, not culture. In this sense sexuality is ontological. By ontology I mean "being." Man was created as a sexual *being*. Sex isn't therefore a development of his ingenuity or intellect or diligence (or biological evolution); it's not a cultural or social construction. Sex (male or female) is hardwired into humanity's very being. Man can no more replace his (or her) sex than he can alter his (or her) mind or conscience. Of course, humans can tamper with and diminish and heighten sex, mind and conscience and many other creational realities. After all, what is sin, but a perversion of God's good creation? Transgender operations can tamper with the physical traits of God-created human sexuality. But they never alter ontology: "Drive out Nature with a pitchfork, she will come back every time" (Horace).[7] Just as man can efface but never erase conscience (Rom. 2:15), so he can modify sex bodily but not ontologically.

Moderns at war with the CSW often see sex as culture, not creation. Sex is engineered reality; you can make sexes just as you can make video games or pecan pies. The term "gender" is deployed to denote a species of sexuality each of us creates and changes almost at will. We are all sexual artists, proving "the unlimited malleability of human sexuality."[8] Ever since humanity's primal sin of rebellion against God's order, men and women have bumped up against the constraints of creation and wished to burst them. "Gender as social construction" is one such striking attempt. Homosexuality, women military combatants, and sex-reassignment surgery are all examples of an anti-CSW. Rod Dreher is quite right, therefore, that gay marriage is not just a social revolution but also a cosmological one.[9] It's man's attempt to reverse- and re-engineer God's creation.

The Bible takes it as a given that humanity as male and female are interdependent but distinct as creational (ontological) realities in which humanity should delight and for whose gift they should worship God.

Sex and Trinity

Second, and following from the first point, man and woman were created in God's image, and the explicit rationale for God's creating woman is that it isn't good for man (male) to be alone (Gen. 2:18). What is it about not being alone that reflects God's image? That answer is easy. God is a Trinity. God is one and he is three. He is three *persons*. "As God is not alone," writes Michael Reeves, "so man in his image should not be alone. [Christians] therefore upheld the physical, femininity, relationship and marriage all as being intrinsically good, created reflections of a God who is not lonely."[10] God created woman not only for procreation (vital, to be sure) but for companionship: God did not make us to be alone, just as he isn't alone. And it's possible that God created Adam first so that he could suffer the pangs of loneliness and appreciate how vital the woman would be to his life (even God alone isn't a sufficient companion for man in creation). The husband and wife share not just their external world but also their inner world. They edify and encourage and bolster one another in times of great hardship (which is inevitable in any marriage). They participate in one another's supreme triumphs and abject defeats.

Today's cult of individualism, therefore, combats the CSW. This cult prizes radical autonomy. The individual and his/her wishes, desires, appetites, dreams, goals, indulgences and aspirations are deemed the summit of "the good life." We have highly personalized playlists on our digital music devices; we encounter a barrage of ads in our web browsing specifically tailored to our previous buying habits and web preferences. We gradually see all of our decisions in light of our own individual benefit and not the benefit of (or consequence to) other people.

More and more, therefore, society is pressured to rely on non-communal resources for happiness (in other words, apart from healthy friendships with other people). Postmodernism, perpetuating a Romantic ideal, has stressed the individual as self-artist:[11] we create (and re-create) ourselves, perhaps many times in a lifetime: this year the rich playboy, next year the New Age acetic, and the year following the religious believer. This month we'll dabble in Christianity and next month Buddhism, next decade a metrosexual, and perhaps later in life, the contemplative sage. What's important is that no external factor hinder what we want to be or become. We are self-creators. We have the *right* to self-creation.

For sex, this means there are no objectives beyond personal gratification and fulfillment. A multiplicity of "partners" and a diversity of experiences are the most logical ways to achieve this objective, and that's the program many individualistic moderns employ. The CSW demands an intimate life shared by a man and woman for an entire lifetime and is the antithesis of an individualistic anti-CSW.

Sex and fruitfulness

One of the explicit reasons God instituted marriage was to perpetuate the human race with God-loving and -fearing descendants (Mal. 2:15). Procreation is a leading (but not the only) reason God instituted sex. God created sex to be such a delightful and even ecstatic experience in order to incentivize and reward the act and process of bringing children into the world. God delights in humans, who are made in his image, and he wants more and more of them with whom to share his Trinitarian communion and to exert benevolent dominion over his creation. When God cursed the sin of woman by making childbearing a painful experience (Gen. 3:16), he was teaching a memorable lesson: sin at the very bringing forth of life blights that which is intended to be good and delightful. Yet, even in sin's curse, God's plan to populate his creation with his image cannot be thwarted, and the joy of a newborn child overcomes the pain of childbirth (Jn. 16:21). The Bible again and again identifies fruitfulness (physical, material, emotional) as one of his blessings (Gen. 17:6; Lev. 26:9; Is. 32:15; Jer. 23:3; Col. 1:10), and children are one of the greatest blessings of all (Ps. 127–128).

God wants his image to perpetuate itself, and he's made it enjoyable and gratifying to do this. Childbearing is a crucial part of the CSW.

Laxity toward or aversion to childbearing and children, therefore, is an aversion to the CSW. The ubiquity of contraception in the West is, to take an example, an evidence of rebellion against God. The Bible doesn't prohibit contraception in all cases. For instance, since the husband's primary obligation is to his wife and not to his (potential) children (Eph. 5:25–28), contraception might be necessary in specific cases to preserve the wife's health. But today's contraception culture didn't begin for such biblically warranted reasons.[12] Rather, it began in an effort to isolate the pleasures of sex from the obligations (for both men and women) of childbearing— "re-creative rather than procreative sex."[13] Sex as gratification (which is not wrong) became the end in itself. The sex act is now an idol.

The contraception culture has yielded to the childless subculture, which in our increased narcissism threatens to become more dominant as a culture.[14] The deliberate choice for couples never to bear children is an act of flagrant rebellion against God, since he longs for more creatures made in his image with whom to share in his communion of Father, Son and Spirit.

An anti-CSW, by contrast, sees children as an intrusion or inconvenience, or at best, an optional reward for an upper-class lifestyle.[15] Children are not understood, as in the CSW, to be both a divine command and blessing nourished in a wholesome and pleasurable sexuality. In the Bible, childlessness is considered a reproach (1 Sam. 1:2–7; Prov. 30:16). In today's culture, children are often deemed a reproach and childlessness a blessing. This approach is a perversion of Christian truth—and it has long-term disastrous social consequences, most notably a lack of sufficient producers of the very benefits needed to sustain a society.[16]

Sex and intimacy

"Therefore a man shall leave his father and his mother and hold fast to his wife, and they shall become one flesh. And the man and his wife were both naked and were not ashamed," writes Moses (Gen. 2:24–25). Only after they sinned did Adam and Eve experience shame at their nakedness (Gen. 3:7–11). They tried to shield themselves both from God and from each other. The nakedness of marriage in Eden exhibited and enhanced the intimacy of a man and woman who love each other enough not to fear sharing their deepest secrets. They have nothing to hide. Even after the Fall, the only relation of a man and a woman in which God permits nakedness is marriage (Lev. 18:5–20). Sin disrupted the intimacy of the human race with one another, but it has been restored in marriage.

The godly husband learns over time how mythical and destructive is the brooding, individualistic male held up as normative in the modern world. He learns that it *not* good for man to be alone—it's positively bad, in fact. He's a half man. The wife by her very nature furnishes the husband a spiritual and emotional and psychological completion—he gets from his wife things that he can get *only* from her, and the most vital is human intimacy and its comforts and security that no man was designed to be without.[17]

The anti-CSW purges intimacy from sex and replaces it with power: the physical power of the male to coerce sex, and the emotional power of the woman to trade sex for something else she actually wants. Men objectify women, and women objectify sex.

Since almost the beginning, sinful humans have commodified sex in the form of (for example) prostitution: men want pleasure, and women want money, without intimacy, both a perversion of the CSW. Anything that a good God can make a sinful man can pervert. The problem is that God has not constructed humanity with the capacity for sex without intimacy. Paul warns, "Do you not know that your bodies are members of Christ? Shall I then take the members of Christ and make them members of a prostitute? Never! Or do you not know that he who is joined to a prostitute becomes one body with her? For, as it is written, 'The two will become one flesh'"(1 Cor. 6:15–16).

Sex creates a one-flesh intimacy, and no matter how casual and mer-cenary the intentions of its recreational practitioners may be, they carry that intimacy and the subsequent relational brokenness of it wherever they go. This is equally a striking warning against premarital sex, and the common (wrong) notion that casual sex has no lasting effects and that one may later settle down and marry with no lingering implications of previous sexual encounters. There is plenty of sex without intended intimacy; there is never sex without actual intimacy, for good or for ill. The anti-CSW may promise pleasure without the blessings and burdens of intimacy, but this promise arrays itself against human ontology, which, as God's design for man, always gets its revenge.

While prostitution has historically been sequestered from society as an embarrassing, if realistic, concession to human sin, the broader commodification of sex that prostitution typifies has become a cultural fact since the Sexual Revolution (SR). As I noted earlier, the reputation of virile young male sexual wolves on campus looking for female conquests that fit into their general aspirations for success and the good life has lately been paralleled by ambitious young female collegians:

> It is by now pretty well understood that traditional dating in college has mostly gone the way of the landline, replaced by "hooking up"—an ambiguous term that can signify anything from making out to oral sex to intercourse—without the emotional entanglement of a relationship.

> Until recently, those who studied the rise of hookup culture had generally assumed that it was driven by men, and that women were reluctant participants, more interested in romance than in casual sexual encounters. But there is an increasing realization that young women are propelling it, too.

> Hanna Rosin, in her recent book, *The End of Men*, argues that hooking up is a functional strategy for today's hard-charging and ambitious young women, allowing them to have enjoyable

sex lives while focusing most of their energy on academic and professional goals.[18]

Since the commodification of sex at the heart of the SR, men have objectified women by trying to sever intimacy from sex. Now women are returning the favor.

Recent assaults on the CSW are driven by assisted reproductive technologies. A leading example is surrogacy, in which a woman carries in her womb another woman's child. This act severs intimacy from fruitfulness. Behind it is often the assumption that children are a human right and not God's gift to be delivered in his prescribed manner.[19] While medical technologies that protect and enhance human life as God intended are a welcome gift at his hands, any reproductive technology that subverts the CSW not merely violates God's moral law but also injures the human condition, no matter how appealing it may be in the short term. SSM, in particular, has an inextricable link with artificial reproductive technologies, since "marriage equality" necessitates the equal right and capacity to reproduce biological offspring—and since this cannot happen in a homosexual relationship according to God's creation ordinance, it must happen artificially. The SR simply cannot reach their desired cultural destination without these technologies.[20]

Sexual intimacy may not be thrown out the window in an effort to get otherwise unavailable children.[21] Children are God's gift—but they must be delivered in his way.

Sex and sacrifice

Paul writes that the husband and wife have no monopoly over their own bodies sexually, but that each has a claim to the other spouse (1 Cor. 7:2–5). This truth explodes the misogyny in traditional cultures in which the bodies of women are possessions for males but not *vice versa*. Paul's main point is that abstinence in marriage is a grievous sin because it defrauds the spouse of what is rightly hers or his: namely, the sexual body and mind and heart of one's spouse. This CSW must sound positively frightful to the ears of moderns (male *and* female) suckled on sexual autonomy: "My body is mine," the same perverse mantra rationalizing abortion. Apart from special times of mutually agreeable fasting and prayer, husbands and wives may not abstain from sex (1 Cor. 7:3–5). Sex within marriage is a godly entitlement that may not be infringed. The husband who avoids spousal sex because he judges his wife unattractive or, worse yet, because his sexual energies are exhausted on porn or other illicit lust is no better than the wife who employs abstinence as a weapon to manipulate her husband.

The choice to marry is the choice to provide sexual pleasure to one's spouse. The erosion of marriage has been both a cause and effect of radical sexual autonomy and consequent self-centeredness that demands sexual gratification apart from sexual sacrifice. In time this autonomy fosters (both figuratively and literally) the masturbation society: sex becomes individualized, which is to say, it becomes no longer sex, since sex by its nature requires a man and a woman.[22]

The CSW is rooted in self-giving: just as the Trinity did not keep that communion to themselves but created human beings to share in it, so also God requires man and woman to sacrifice themselves in marriage, including in sex, to manifest the self-giving character of God.

Sex and complementarity

Camille Paglia rocked the urbane feminist world with her iconoclastic 1990 *Sexual Personae*.[23] She argued that the bland egalitarian sexuality of Western liberalism is an unrealistic sublimation of the uncontrollable primitive sexual urges so evident in nature-paganism: (violent) creation at war on (domesticated) culture. Because she denies the creational truth of the CSW, Paglia sees only competition, never complementarity, between man and woman in their sexuality.[24] The CSW is nearly the opposite: man's sinful culture is at war with God's good creation. Ancient pagan nature worship glorified and exploited the differences between the sexes for sordid, perverse purposes, while ancient pagan spirituality tried to overcome the differences altogether in its program of monist "one-ism": deity and humanity are one in nature, a unity reaching its apex in homosexuality.[25] The CSW recognizes difference between man and woman, but it's a difference of complementarity, not competition.

Man and woman are both made in God's image, but each is distinctive and, in fact, distinctive in ways that correspond to—complement — each other. God fashioned woman to be different from man in the very ways that correspond to his inherent male limitations. Quite literally, Genesis teaches us that when God brought Eve to Adam, he met his match.[26] God created woman to *match* man. He created her to be man's precise counterpart—to fulfill exactly those areas in which God created man lacking. In short, God created man not to survive without his counterpart, the woman. God created man incomplete. Adam was created good, like the rest of creation. He was not, however, created fully fulfilled in himself. Just as creation was created good but needed man and woman's loving cultivation, so the man was created good, but needed the woman as counterpart. The sexual differences between men and women rooted in the creation order highlight God's intention that neither man nor woman was created to be alone.

We complementarians are sometimes accused of embracing the superiority of men. That charge is frankly, and ironically, false. If anything, we recognize the superiority of women in most matters of life. They're often more faithful, more nurturing, more thoughtful, more creative, more insightful, more provident, and more sacrificial. We simply recognize that men are superior in a few limited ways (military combat, church leadership, physical athletics, and so forth).

To argue against sexual equality is not to argue for across-the-board superiority or inferiority. It is to argue for *both* superiority *and* inferiority, and for *both* men *and* women, one or the other, depending on the situation.

Modern sexual egalitarianism does not succeed in erasing these differences; after all, fighting creation is fighting God. Sexual egalitarianism only succeeds in frustrating men and women: it disrupts the creation order that God intended for both men and women's enjoyment.

Nor is sexual egalitarianism merely a private and individualized matter. It is the primal dimension of political utopianism. This politically egalitarian impulse is especially striking in the practice of homosexuality.[27] To the denizens of the left, it became increasingly evident in the 20th century that economic egalitarianism was not sufficient: "Progressive political change was doomed to failure unless it was accompanied by the abolition of sexual repression."[28] The truly just society required sexual leveling, not merely economic leveling. This leveling included, but could not be limited to, feminism.[29] The SR was simply the most intimate component of left-wing politics and the left-wing worldview. That component included (1) "the explosion of youth culture (and the student political movements) that stimulated the thirst of young men and women for sexual experience before marriage"; (2) feminism; and, finally, (3) the gay liberation movement.[30]

In the end, left-wing politics simply became the cultural vehicle for delivering pervasively egalitarian sexual practices. It finally dawned on leftists that it was culture, not politics, that they really wanted to change.[31]

SSM is a particular culprit of leftist political utopianism, since the actual (in distinction from stated) goal of leading SSM advocates is the abolition of marriage, a social "buffer" against naked state power, so that the state gains unhampered social authority.[32] Far from assuring individual liberty, SSM undermines the very institution (the family) that guards against state encroachment that prevails whenever competing institutions are conquered by radical social engineering. For this reason, it is counterintuitive when libertarians support SSM; it expands the size and scope of the state. SSM doesn't contract state power and intrusion.

The radical anti-CSW links promiscuity, premarital sex, feminism, recreational contraception, homosexuality, and same-sex marriage. Each in its own way destroys God-established hierarchies. Promiscuity erodes the sanctity of the family. Premarital sex assaults the exclusiveness of the marriage bed. Feminism degrades women by leveling the divinely established noble female calling highlighted in the differences between men and women. Recreational contraception sacrifices the solemn bond between sexual intercourse and children on the altar of personal gratification. Homosexuality abolishes altogether either the male or the female in the sexual union. Same-sex marriage legally codifies this radical, God-defying egalitarianism by simply redefining—that is, rescinding—marriage. Each of these acts subverts divine hierarchies given for humanity's flourishing under God's glory.

Conclusion

Imagine, if you will, a strange architectural student who thought he could use a word processing software program to create a highly technical architectural schematic. No matter how hard he tried, or how frustrated he became, he would fail. He would fail because the operating system of a word processing program was never designed to create architectural schematics. The software writer had nothing whatsoever like architectural design in mind when he devised the program. He didn't even include the basic digital building blocks by which one could alter the word processing program in order to make it an architectural design program. People, even well-intentioned people, who try to use the word processing program for something other than processing words are doomed to failure. Always.

Similarly, human sexuality is a vital aspect of God's design for humanity. God designed sexuality to be loving, intimate, sacrificial, enjoyable, and productive (literally!). It was designed to be what we nowadays term heterosexual. Intercourse was designed exclusively for marriage. We are aware of this sexual design not merely by deduction from the created personhood but also by reading God's revelation in the Bible. God tells us what his design was, and he *shows* us what it was.

Christian sexual ethics are not obsolete and can never become obsolete in God's created world because they're a part of his created reality. This sexual design could be abolished as easily as God's entire creation could be abolished. The anti-CSW so pervasive in Western culture, therefore, is doomed to failure. That is to say, it is doomed to fail in its attempt to alter humanity's sexuality. It is not doomed to failure, however, in creating widespread psychological depression, wrecked marriages, murdered pre-born children, sexual addictions, the objec-tification of women, the emasculation of men, the abuse of children, the reduction of childbearing, and the rootlessness of teenagers and young adults. Each of these is a bitter—and palpable—fruit of mod-ern man's mad, autonomous, rebellious quest to throw off the alleged repression of Christian sexual ethics. We in Western culture have lived a good many years now under the cultural and legal imposition of this great liberation project. The tree was planted, it has matured, and its harvests confront us. The bitter fruit of those harvests now surround us—in our families, churches, schools, politics, hospitals, boardrooms, courtrooms, and therapists' offices. The verdict is in, and it is far from pleasant.

Insanity, it is held, consists of doing the same thing and expecting different results. We live in a sexually insane culture. As spiritually and psychologically painful as it will be to turn back from our socially habituated insanity, only by sane recovery of Christian sexual ethics can Western culture expect a cure to the deep maladies that presently infect us.

Endnotes to Chapter 4

1   David Naugle, *Worldview: The History of a Concept* (Grand Rapids: Eerdmans, 2002), 9.

2   James H. Olthius, "On Worldviews," *Christian Scholars Review*, Vol. XIV, No. 2 (1985), 155.

3   Linda Hirshman, *Victory: The Triumphant Gay Revolution* (New York: HarperCollins, 2012), 72.

4   David F. Wells, *The Courage to be Protestant* (Grand Rapids: Eerdmans, 2008), 45.

5   John M. Frame, *The Doctrine of the Christian Life* (Phillipsburg, NJ: P & R, 2008), 854.

6   Cornelius Van Til, *The Defense of the Faith* (Phillipsburg, NJ: Presbyterian and Reformed, 1967 edition), 49.

7   Edmund A. Walsh, *The Fall of the Russian Empire* (New York: Blue Ribbon Books, 1928), 5.

8   Theodore Dalrymple, "All Sex, All the Time," *Our Culture, What's Left of It* (Chicago: Ivan R. Dee, 2005), 248.

9   Rod Dreher, "Sex After Christianity," http://theamericanconservative.com/articles/sex-after-christianity/. Accessed August 13, 2014.

10   Michael Reeves, *The Good God* (Milton Keynes, England: Paternoster, 2012), 37.

11   Charles Guignon, *Being Authentic* (London and New York: Routledge, 2004), 49–77. Special thanks to my son and colleague Richard A. Sandlin for recommending this source.

12   Mary Eberstadt, *Adam and Eve After the Pill* (San Francisco: Ignatius Press, 2012), 134–158.

13   *Ibid.*, 55.

14   Lauren Sandler, "The Childfree Life: When Having It All Means Not Having Children," *Time*, August 12, 2013, 38–45.

15   Charles Murray, *Coming Apart* (New York: Crown Forum, 2012), 149–167.

16   David DesRosiers, "Book Review: 'What to Expect When No One's

Expecting,'" http://washingtontimes.com/news/2013/mar/4/book-review-what-to-expect-when-no-ones-expecting/. Accessed February 8, 2014.

17 Not all men were designed by God to be married, but those who were not require a special grace from God to compensate for the lack of intimacy of marriage (Mt. 19:12; 1 Cor. 7:7).

18 Kate Taylor, "Sex on Campus: She Can Play That Game Too," http://nytimes.com/2013/07/14/fashion/sex-on-campus-she-can-play-that-game-too.html. Accessed July 12, 2013.

19 Jennifer Lahl , "The Overlooked Ethics of Reproduction," http://christianitytoday.com/women/2013/august/overlooked-ethics-of-reproduction.html. Accessed February 8, 2014. See also John M. Frame, *The Doctrine of the Christian Life*, 788.

20 Michael Hanby, "The Brave New World of Same-Sex Marriage," http://thefederalist.com/2014/02/19/the-brave-new-world-of-same-sex-marriage/. Accessed August 13, 2014.

21 Adoption, which the Bible permits (Ex. 2:10; Est. 2:7), is in a different category altogether. It does not intentionally sever intimacy from fruitfulness. It ameliorates an already broken situation.

22 Masturbation represents a separate category from, e.g., fornication. It clearly fails God's design for sex between a man and woman, but it isn't condemned in the Bible. (Onan, in Gen. 38 is sometimes offered as a counter-example, but God's judgment was leveled on him not for masturbation but for violating God's law in refusing to furnish a seed to his deceased, childless brother's house.) Francis A. Schaeffer offers this balanced assessment: "The Bible does not . . . give a clear command against masturbation. I think, therefore, it does two things at once. It clearly shows that the only proper solution [for sexual practice] is in the one-man, one-woman relationship. And yet it does not give an explicit negative concerning masturbation, and thus puts it in a different category than adultery, fornication, and so on. I feel that this is the reason that it is handled as it is in the Bible—that is, that it does both things at once," in *Letters of Francis A. Schaeffer* (Westchester, IL: Crossway, 1985), 243.

23 Camille Paglia, *Sexual Personae* (New York: Vintage, 1990, 1991).

24 *Ibid.*, 25–36.

25 Peter Jones, *One or Two: Seeing a World of Difference* (Escondido, CA: Main

Entry Editions, 2010), 169–183.

26 Marvin R. Wilson, *Father Abraham* (Grand Rapids: Eerdmans, 1989), 201.

27 Jeffrey Escoffier, "Emancipation, Sexual Liberation, and Identity Politics," *New Politics*, Vol. XI, No. 5 (Summer 2008), 38–43.

28 *Ibid.*, 41.

29 It includes androgyny, the socially constructed blended-male-female being. The agenda for its normalization has been driven by political radicalism. See Allan Carson, "The Androgyny Hoax," *Persuasion at Work*, Vol. 9, No. 2 (March, 1986), 1–10.

30 Jeffrey Escoffier, "Emancipation, Sexual Liberation, and Identity Politics," 39. Escoffier observes, further, that "changes in the social forms organizing sexuality and gender relations — for example, invention of the birth control pill, large-scale entry of married women into the labor force, decline of the family wage, increased divorce rates, and the emergence of a new consumerism — played a role in the sexual revolution."

31 Richard Wolin, *The Wind from the East* (Princeton and Oxford: Princeton University Press, 2010), 350–370.

32 Stella Morabito, "Bait And Switch: How Same Sex Marriage Ends Family Autonomy," http://thefederalist.com/2014/04/09/bait-and-switch-how-same-sex-marriage-ends-marriage-and-family-autonomy/. Accessed August 13, 2014.

Chapter 5

Christian Responsibility in Sexually Chaotic Times

The dramatic and swift success in Western culture of the Sexual Revolution (SR), particularly exhibited in same-sex marriage (SSM), has guaranteed the present evaporation of the Christian sexual worldview (CSW) in our world. Christians should neither shut their eyes to the reality of this tragic loss nor despair that they can do nothing to reverse it. Rather, they should confront it realistically and consider a principled response in light of that reality. What are the leading features of that reality?

Hard Realism in Sexually Chaotic Times

The collapse of plausibility structures

First, we are witnessing the collapse of a massive "plausibility structure." By "plausibility structure," I mean what Peter Berger has described as a humanly constructed coercive objectivity that has gained the "power to constitute and to impose itself as a reality."[1] For thousands of years of human history what marriage *is* was taken for granted. Throughout its history it has been assaulted, injured, and diluted—but never redefined. The fact that the West in recent years is the first civilization in human history to redefine marriage verifies our apostasy. Our civilization was shaped by both Christian culture and the Greco-Roman world. Christianity has been unwaveringly opposed to homosexuality. The sophisticated paganism of Greece and Rome, unlike Christianity, was lax about homosexuality—but not about the definition of marriage: "[E]ven in cultures very favorable to homoerotic relationships (as in ancient Greece), something akin to the conjugal ["traditional"] view has prevailed—nothing like same-sex marriage was even imagined."[2] The definition was no different in the East and Orient or any other culture. In creating SSM, our civilization is, therefore, overthrowing the entire history of humanity's definition of marriage. Our depravity isn't merely substantive; it's also structural. We're not merely evil; we're creating principles and institutions for the purpose of enshrining our evil. SSM is becoming a new plausibility structure.

When plausibility structures collapse, an entire way of thinking and, therefore, of acting in a culture changes. The transition between the collapse of the old and the adoption of the new creates, for a time at least, a deep cultural unsettledness springing from conceptual conflicts to which humans are simply not accustomed. In the case of SSM, the conflict isn't hard to demonstrate. Quick: what's marriage? The fact that you fumbled mentally at a definition you could articulate (as opposed to merely intuitively assume) doesn't prove that there is no workable definition for marriage or that it's a hard concept to understand. It only proves that marriage has been a plausibility structure for so long that nobody thought about defining it. Is it a legal contract between any man and woman? No, because such contracts occur every day and nobody would call them a marriage. Is marriage a long-term sexually committed relationship between a man and woman? Nobody would call that a marriage either. What about commitment to long-term fidelity (however defined) before witnesses secured by a state-sanctioned marriage license? This would disqualify most of what were considered marriages throughout human history.

The reason we're obliged to re-think these definitions (or think about them in the first place) is that nobody before recent times would have even considered that people of the same sex could marry. SSM wouldn't have been deemed so much immoral as implausible; we would have lacked the conceptual equipment with which to envision such a scenario.

Another example in the last century was the (re-)definition of personhood in the Third Reich. A chief objective of the Nazi propaganda machine under the undisputed direction of Joseph Goebbels was to dehumanize (literally) the Jewish population so that the rest of society would accept their enslavement and eventual liquidation. In time, that objective worked. This transformation required a deep unsettledness, overturning as it did centuries of the Western plausibility structure of personhood defined as man created in God's image and entitled to basic humane [!] treatment. To be *biologically* human was *ipso facto* to be entitled to *spiritual* personhood. The Nazis changed that formulation for the Jews, and that change, while successful, wasn't easy. Its unsettledness is captured in an exchange in the classic movie *Schindler's List*, based on the true story of German entrepreneur and war profiteer Oscar Schindler, who over time became horrified at the Nazi extermination machine and used his war-labor factories to shield Jews from it. In one scene, Itzhak Stern, Schindler's Jewish assistant played by Ben Kingsley, quibbles with Schindler on the most effective words to use on Schindler's list of names scheduled to be submitted to the Nazis to assure his Jewish workers would be considered worthy of not being exterminated.

In exasperation, Schindler retorts, "Must we invent a whole new language?"

"I think so, yes," Stern responds quietly.

Collapsing plausibility structures demand replacement plausibility structures, and since all such structures presuppose concepts and language for converting those concepts, no collapse survives without conceptual and linguistic unsettledness.

Today we speak of "traditional marriage" versus "same-sex marriage." A century ago this linguistic juxtaposition would have been as incomprehensible as if we today spoke of "traditional wars" versus "non-violent wars," or "traditional widowers" versus "married widowers." Some plausibility structures are so inflexible and deep-seated and their meaning so self-evident that redefining them seems tautological. The fact that we today can speak of "traditional marriage" and "same-sex marriage" testifies to the nearly unprecedented success of the radical homosexual agenda in unseating a millennia-long marital plausibility structure that has never had a single competitor in any culture anywhere.

Whatever we may say of SSM, it transports us into uncharted territory. We have no idea what a non-heterosexual marital plausibility structure would—or even could—look like.

Holistic apostasy

Second, SSM is simply the latest in a series of breathtaking cultural deviations spawned by the wholesale abandonment of biblical faith in the West. We mustn't make the mistake of seeing SSM as a stand-alone issue that Christians must combat with stand-alone techniques. SSM isn't even merely one aspect of a broader apostasy ignited by the SR.[3] Rather, it is a logical sequence in an entire chain of apostate reasoning. Leftism since the French Revolution has engaged in one big emancipation project, what Kenneth Minogue terms "the oppression-liberation nexus."[4] The leftist religion has become one of clawing for the liberation of humanity from every tyranny—real or imagined: the secularists must be emancipated from the religionists, the parishioners from the clergy, the enlightened from the unenlightened, the citizens from royalty, the poor from the rich, the workers from the capitalists, blacks from whites, women from men, wives from husbands, children from parents, debtors from creditors, employees from employers, homosexuals from heterosexuals, convicts from law-abiding citizens, and soon, if the trajectory persists, polygamists from monogamists and pedophiles from prison guards. The Great Emancipation now extends even to non-human nature: the emancipation of "the environment" from a rapacious humanity. The "oppression-liberation nexus" has become such a successful program that we cannot make sense of the last few centuries without it. SSM, which levels marriage to legally recognized monogamous homosexuality (the inclusion of incestuous, polyamorous and pedophilic relationships comes next) is at the moment the controversial cutting edge of its merciless saber that has since the French Revolution annihilated every perceived cultural hierarchy.[5] This saber cuts a broad and deep swath, and its work is far from finished.

The bankruptcy of secular defenses of marriage

Third, while Christians welcome specific secular arguments for marriage that contribute to sound public policy, our civilization can't eventually avoid a head-on clash between the CSW and non-Christian sexual ethics as they play themselves out in our culture. The problem with secular arguments for sexual ethics (including arguments for "traditional marriage") is that they spring from the same root as arguments for SSM: human autonomy. Able secular proponents of "traditional marriage" argue for "the common good" and "human flourishing"— only marriage gives us happy, well-balanced children; strong family bonds; and useful citizens. The problem is that many advocates of homosexuality see a society that discriminates against SSM as *not* a "common good," and, even were they to grant that "traditional marriage" fosters more well-adjusted families, they would still insist that a sexually discriminatory society must be abolished. For them, the right of homosexuals to marry is part of "the common good." For these homosexuals and their heterosexual allies, what constitutes "good" is not held in "common" with "traditional" marriage advocates. It's not, therefore, "the common good" or "human flourishing" to which Christians must ultimately appeal, but to the word of God.

Therefore, the Christian stake in the SSM debate isn't merely to preserve marriage as an institution—it's to recover the biblical worldview and its religious presuppositions that demand marriage. Sexual ethics are a single cloth woven of many strands, and to remove one is eventually to unravel the entire cloth. The Enlightenment got rid of the Bible as binding revelation. Romanticism elevated the individual's feelings and emotions as paramount to the "authentic" life. Existentialism resituated ethics as human choice. Postmodernity and multiculturalism undermined "meta-narratives," including ethical and sexual meta-narratives, and glorified moral relativism. Pluralism installed the libertarian ethic expressed most pointedly in the aphorism: "I'm OK and you're OK, as long as your OK doesn't infringe on my OK." In such an ideational climate, rife on TV and the Internet and in elementary schools and universities and in pop culture and, yes, too often in the church, SSM is a logical and reasonable social and legal fact. Indeed, *not* to have SSM in such a climate would be odd and counterintuitive. SSM isn't compatible with Christian sexual ethics, but it is fully compatible with the guiding presuppositions and plausibility structures of Western civilization in the 21st century.

In the end, there can be no convincing argument for marriage and against SSM not rooted in religious presuppositions disclosed in creation and crystallized in the Bible. Therefore, the task of Christians committed (as they must be) to the CSW is a robust gospel life—the Christian worldview summarized in the creation-fall-redemption paradigm.[6] We must tell and show our sin-sick world that God's way isn't simply the best way among many, but the only way that doesn't end in civilizational degradation and eternal damnation. Christian sexual ethics aren't repressive—they're beautiful, because a loving God's way is infinitely preferable to a sinful man's way of ordering man's world.

We've tried man's sexual ethics for several generations now. Amid rampant divorce and broken families and fatherless children and the objectification of women and sex-minus-love college students and "gender" chaos, how about *Christian* sexual ethics in our culture? If so, how does the church do this? *Should* the church do it?

The Church's Responsibility in Sexually Chaotic Times

Some devout Christians answer no. In his sermon "Taking Refuge: Reflections on Same-Sex Marriage,"[7] Senior Pastor Dan Scott of Christ Church-Nashville presents as lucid, logical, and thoughtful a case for the church to abandon the "culture wars" in light of the impending full-fledged victory of the SSM agenda as any other Christian leader in the United States has offered. Christ Church-Nashville is a prominent evangelical, charismatic and liturgical (ancient-future[8]) church, and Scott's conclusions represent a serious engagement with SSM that many other Christians have adopted in whole or in part. But to those of us committed to a full-fledged biblical faith, several of those strategic and tactical conclusions are mistaken, and they warrant consideration since they are likely to appeal to many Christians in our sexually chaotic times.

First, I must note that Pastor Scott asserts a number of entirely legitimate facts: that many American Christians have been more interested in patriotism and civil religion than biblical Christianity; that the evangelical church has generally mimicked the world, simply following its lead but merely a few years behind its trends; that homosexuality is non-biblical, and that "[i]nterpretations of those [biblical] passages that affirm something different than [i.e., passages traditionally understood to prohibit homosexuality] are very, very new and very, very suspicious"; that the church has often resisted the prohibition not only of homosexual misbehavior but also heterosexual misbehavior; that all Christians, not merely homosexuals in the church, need grace and forgiveness; that "the church claims to be an institution that proclaims eternal truths about life and eternity," including eternal truths about human sexuality; that legal homosexual unions (SSM) are not, in fact, marriages; that the American church cannot persist in following the culturally conditioned, revivalistic "old-time religion" of the American frontier, which, in any case, "is not really that old"; and that the church must be more interested in fidelity than in relevance. In these assertions and others, Scott presents a biblically warranted and prophetic paradigm for the church in sexually chaotic times.

Marriage as a holy institution in culture

But he says much more, and some of what he says, particularly his paradigm for the church amid the wholesale legalization of SSM, warrants scrutiny. Scott writes, for example, of the summer 2013 Supreme Court decisions effectively opening the gates for SSM:

> What the Supreme Court rulings destroyed was our ability to view the country as a kind of church, where nonbelievers are welcome but expected to conform to the minimal moral standards of our faith. If we had any doubts about that before, perhaps we lost them this week. The nation is not a church. Non-Christian citizens do not intend to live by the teachings of our faith, including what we believe about marriage....
>
> The place to begin perhaps is to note how Christians ideally view and experience marriage. Christians believe that marriage begins as a ceremonial and sacramental event. It is something we have traditionally called Holy Matrimony. This event is not primarily a photo opportunity, a way to celebrate what has actually been done by the state. For a Christian, a marriage license from the state is merely a legal recognition of a Christian sacrament. Thus, the sacred covenant two Christians make in the sacrament of Holy Matrimony is not with the state; but with God. We appropriately ask the state to recognize the bond that results from the sacramental act of Holy Matrimony

in order to establish the legitimacy of certain legal rights and privileges that our society grants to married partners....

Non-Christians establish a marriage contract through other religious ceremonies or through a secular registration of their intention to live together as a couple. In that sense, Christians and non-Christians use the same word – marriage – to define two different concepts....

In this light, what the Supreme Court decided this week was that our states are now free to extend legal recognition of the contractual bonds traditionally made by heterosexual couples to homosexuals. States have not, and cannot, redefine what constitutes the sacrament of Holy Matrimony....

A critical error in this approach is Scott's anchoring marriage as an institution in the Christian church when biblically it is displayed as a creation ordinance (Gen. 2:23–25).

Marriage is a pre-redemptive, creational ordinance, not first a redemptive, Christian ordinance. Grace, indeed, perfects nature, and our Lord's redemption elevates marriage;[9] but marriage predates both the church and state, and God's revelation governing it transcends his revelation governing the church and state. Referring to marriage by the traditional language of "Holy Matrimony" is a superb rhetorical move in a society that wishes to secularize marriage, but only as long as it reminds us that biblical standards for a holy marriage are wider than the church and can never be limited to it.

In short, the state, not simply the church, must recognize holy standards. Marriage is holy not because it is a church ordinance, but because it is a *divine* ordinance. This is why the church has always recognized and must always recognize marriages among non-church unbelievers, not simply Christian and church-based marriages. And the church rightly doesn't recognize SSM, not because it's outside the church, but because it isn't marriage.

Scott is quite correct when he observes that "the sacred covenant two Christians make in the sacrament of Holy Matrimony is not with the state; but with God"; yet he could have said the same thing about the church. Both state and church *recognize* marriage. Neither is a *party* to the covenant. Marriage is a two-dimensional covenant (1) between a man and woman (Mal. 2:14) and (2) between the spouses and God (Mt. 19:6). Church and state enhance and enforce the marriage covenant in ways appropriate to the sphere of each. The church bolsters the marriage by the means of grace (Eph. 5:21–33), and the state protects the marriage by means of lawful coercion (Rom. 13:1–7—assuring parents' care for their children, for example).

It's mistaken, therefore, to conclude that for Christian and non-Christian, marriage is "two different concepts." No doubt non-believers often don't consider marriage in the way Christians do, any more than they consider the state the way Christians do, but this difference of opinion has nothing to do with the institutional definition of marriage any more than the institutional definition of the state. Christians may not affirm two mutually contradictory definitions of the state simply because non-Christians don't agree with them, and they may not do the same thing with marriage, either. Marriage is no less a "sacred covenant" (Scott's language) between unbelievers than it is between believers. Subjective unbelief doesn't invalidate marriage's covenant objectivity.

Scott is on track, then, to write, "States have not, and cannot, redefine what constitutes the sacrament of Holy Matrimony," if he means to say that the state cannot define or redefine marriage. But if he means to say that the state may impute the term "marriage" to same-sex unions as long as they're not Christian, he's greatly mistaken. Every married person partakes of Holy Matrimony, and it doesn't become less holy merely because a justice of the peace presides over the covenant making.

It's the institution that's holy, not the parties to it. That's why we call it Holy Matrimony, not Holy Husbands and Wives.

Is homosexuality merely one sin among many?

Not only does Pastor Scott posit two differing concepts of marriage. He levels out the significance of homosexuality in relation to other sexual sins: "What I am hoping to establish here is that homosexual behavior is not of a different magnitude of sin than inappropriate heterosexual behavior. Furthermore, homosexual behavior is not more damaging than many non-sexual sins that churches tolerate or even celebrate." If homosexuality is not of greater magnitude than nonmarital fornication, it's strange that God imposed the death penalty for it in the Mosaic legislation (Lev. 18:22; 20:13) and that Paul identifies it as the ultimate sin God allows to be unleashed on an apostate culture (Rom. 1:22–28). All sexual sin is evil, but some sins are of a "different magnitude" than others (see Mt. 12:31). Any sin renders us a law-breaker and exposes us to God's judgment (Jas. 2:10), but that fact doesn't equalize all sins.

A problem with equalizing homosexuality is that it readily leads to a logic which diminishes its severity: "Well, yes, homosexuality is wrong, but so is sleeping around by Christian teens, and we all know that everybody does *that*, so let's just be patient and hope the whole lot of them change." This isn't Pastor Scott's view, but equalizing homosexuality easily permits that kind of (sinful) logic.

Are we called simply to "manage" same-sex attraction?

Third, and similarly, Scott equalizes same-sex attraction and (illicit) heterosexual attraction. The Bible prohibits sexual lust, of course (Mt. 5:28), but while heterosexual lust (sinfully) springs from legitimate and regulated sexual attraction, homosexual lust springs from perverted sexual attraction. The fact that the Bible *lacks any category for regulating homosexual desires and acts* as it does so extensively with heterosexual desires and acts refutes the notion that they are ever valid. In the Bible, homosexuality, like bestiality and incest, is simply condemned, never regulated. Homosexual lust, unlike heterosexual lust, is never regulated. There is simply no place for it. Scott writes:

> Sexual desire goes where it goes, and we must learn to manage it. Thankfully, few people, except for the most wealthy and famous, can act out all the fantasies in their heads. That includes many Christians who are presently, or who have at some time been, attracted to a person of their same sex. Sexual desire comes and goes, perhaps causes embarrassment or pain and then goes away, at least for a while. Most of us are in the same boat that way. I'll assure you it doesn't go away completely until some time well after one's sixtieth birthday.

But sexual desire isn't an impersonal force, like wind or water. It's the conscious choice of sinful human beings: "Let no one say when he is tempted, 'I am being tempted by God,' for God cannot be tempted with evil, and he himself tempts no one. But each person is tempted when he is lured and enticed by his own desire. Then desire when it has conceived gives birth to sin, and sin when it is fully grown brings forth death" (Jas. 1:13–15). Temptation (including sexual temptation) is a satanic lure. Pastor Scott paints a bleak scenario for vanquishing lust, but the Bible teaches that by the Spirit's power, we can overcome this sin, even if never perfectly in this life, not simply "manage" it (Rom. 6:1–18; 1 Jn. 3:1–9).[10] All illicit lust (including homosexual lust) leads to eternal death, according to James, if we don't vanquish it. The reason Christians fall into homosexuality is that they fall into homosexual lust—just as Christians fall into illicit heterosexuality because they fall into heterosexual lust. Lust is always precedent. A tolerant attitude toward lust paves the way for sinful sexual acts, whether heterosexual or homosexual.

The high cost of abandoning the cultural battlefield

Pastor Scott draws his argument to a conclusion by laying out a rationale for the church to abandon the cultural battlefield, notably on homosexuality and SSM, and to narrow its focus to modeling Christian families in the church:

> Furthermore, I have given up the culture war. I am not embracing all aspects of contemporary culture, but I am not at war with contemporary culture. I just don't think we can serve people and fight them at the same time. We cannot talk about traditional marriage by becoming hostile to gay people. We will make a convincing case for biblical marriage if we offer the world some examples of successful and loving Christian marriages....

> We [in the church] pray for the sick. We feed the hungry. We encourage the discouraged. If we do that, we don't have time to fight the nation or its leaders, and at any rate, they too need the love of God.

> We must settle ourselves. For the truth is, eras of history come and go. It is only God who remains eternally constant and certain. If we will not become militant and hostile, the Eternal God will "speak peace to our soul." He will show us what the song means that promises, "in every change, He faithful will remain."

Scott offers an either/or solution to the SR: either oppose it *or* offer biblical alternatives to it. He should have offered a *both/and*. He doesn't believe this is possible: "I just don't think we can serve people and fight them at the same time." He seems to be confusing categories. It's possible to serve people and simultaneously fight *the sin and its agenda* to which they're committed. This after all, is what the gospel is all about, and to say we cannot serve people and fight them—if what he really means, and seems to mean, is to fight the culturally popular sin to which they're enslaved—is to deny the possibility of gospel preaching, not only cultural reclamation, which is a subset of gospel preaching. The gospel is about fighting sin and about God's way of getting rid of it (Romans 1–11 makes this abundantly clear). The same is true of God's way of reclaiming culture. If you want to serve people without fighting their sin, you're not serving them.

So Scott is on solid biblical footing when he argues that the church fails if it fights cultural evil while not concurrently modeling "successful and loving Christian marriage." But modeling the truth isn't a sufficient tactic for Christian living in an evil culture. It's necessary, but not sufficient. Noah and Moses and Isaiah and Hosea and Malachi and John the Baptist and Peter and Paul—and Jesus—exposed ("fought") the cultural evils of their time. Not merely the churchly evils, mind you, but the cultural evils. Noah was a "preacher of righteousness" (2 Pet. 2:5) to an apostate culture. Isaiah exposed the sins not only of Israel but also the surrounding nations (see ch. 15–21). John the Baptist confronted the fornication of a popular politician (Mk. 6:17–18). Paul pulled back the curtain on the cultural depravity of both Gentiles and Jews (Rom. 1–2). Each was a cultural warrior. Not one limited his confrontation of sin to the proverbial four walls of the church. Not one employed a *sola ecclesia* (church alone) strategy in opposing sin and championing righteousness.

The cultural mandate mandates culture wars

Behind the "culture wars" lies a foundational biblical premise: that man's creational calling is to steward the earth for God's glory (Gen. 1:26–28). Man is God's deputy in stewarding the entire created order to bring all glory to him. We denote this calling the "cultural mandate." This means that God's interests are larger than the church, and that, consequently, man's calling is wider than the church. The church is God's agency for propagating the gospel and discipling the nations and edifying the saints and protecting and perpetuating orthodoxy (1 Tim. 3:15), but it's not the kingdom of God, which is the reign of God in the earth.[11] The church is only one aspect (though a vital aspect) of that kingdom. Reducing man's calling to the church is to surrender vast reaches of the world to satanic reign, the kingdom of Satan. This kingdom vies for the same territory as the kingdom of God. This is also why Jesus commanded his disciples to pray that God's will be done on earth as it is in heaven (Mt. 6:10). On earth, not just in the church.

The problem of Scott's *sola ecclesia* strategy runs deeper still. If Jesus Christ isn't Lord everywhere (Acts. 2:22–36), he soon won't be Lord anywhere. To retreat into the church and erect a firewall against sinful culture and declare oneself "not at war with contemporary culture" with the hope that the church will thereby preserve its holiness won't protect the church. Satan is rapacious, a roaring lion (1 Pet. 5:8), the first and ultimate boundary-violator (Gen. 3). He will not leave the church in peace just as long as the church leaves the culture in peace. Sin and righteousness are mutually exclusive and fundamentally irreconcilable; each is by its nature must root out the other. One will be servant and one will be master (Rom. 6:16). Sin won't be satisfied with cultural hegemony; it wants to destroy everything godly and pure and holy, and that includes the church and its marriages.

This means that any strategy for opposing sin that limits that opposition to only one sphere of life is doomed to failure. Sin is too powerful to resist any opposition but full-fledged evisceration. God is in the sin-evisceration business, not the sin-marginalization business.

Churches that wish to preserve "successful and loving Christian marriages" but refuse to stand against unsuccessful and unloving—and perverted—definitions of marriage in the culture will soon discover those depraved marriages beating down the church doors. This is as much as to say that cultural transformation by the power of the gospel

is essential to preserve the long-term health of the church, and that a
strategy of church renewal alone as the means to cultural renewal is
doomed to failure. The course of the church in 20th century Western
culture hasn't been the successful protection of its walls from increasing incursion by social depravity. All to the contrary: as the church
abandoned its earlier Reformational paradigm of active cultural engagement,[12] it gradually accommodated itself to the increasing cultural
depravity surrounding it.

When, therefore, Pastor Scott declares, "We hope our nation will
grow in godliness, but it is far more important that believers and the
church grow in godliness," he creates an unnecessary antithesis. If
Christians refuse to confront evils in the culture, we will soon confront them with a vengeance in the church.

In his conclusion, Pastor Scott urges his listeners and readers to
"take refuge" "in the teachings of Jesus." What biblical Christian
will argue with this exhortation? But the Jesus in whom we must
take refuge, along with his teaching, is not merely Savior; he's also
Lord. And he's not Lord only of the church; he's Lord of all things.
As Lord of all things, he's progressively trampling down evil in his
present, post-resurrection reign (1 Cor. 15:22–25), and even though
the days are dark, and we don't yet see all things subordinated to him
(Heb. 2:8c–9), we join with our Lord in stewarding his earth for
his glory. This stewardship doesn't stop (or start) at the four walls of
the church, and if we want to vanquish the SR, and its most flagrant
recent manifestation of SSM, we had better steward widely indeed.

The priestly church

Churchly obligation includes prophetic and kingly callings, not
simply a priestly one. Priests in the new covenant are ambassadors
for Jesus Christ:

All this is from God, who through Christ reconciled us to

himself and gave us the ministry of reconciliation; that is, in Christ God was reconciling the world to himself, not counting their trespasses against them, and entrusting to us the message of reconciliation. Therefore, we are ambassadors for Christ, God making his appeal through us. We implore you on behalf of Christ, be reconciled to God. (2 Cor. 5:18–20)

The church doesn't mediate salvation (only Jesus does that [1 Tim. 2:5]), but the church is God's main locus for putting sinners into contact with that mediation. The church of the new covenant (like Israel in the old covenant [Ex. 19:6]) is God's priestly people.

The prophetic church

But the church constitutes God's prophetic people as well. Old covenant Israel was the steward of the oracles of God (Rom. 3:1–2), his law, which other nations would contemplate with awe and wonder:

Keep them [God's laws] and do them, for that will be your wisdom and your understanding in the sight of the peoples, who, when they hear all these statutes, will say, 'Surely this great nation is a wise and understanding people.' For what great nation is there that has a god so near to it as the LORD our God is to us, whenever we call upon him? And what great nation is there, that has statutes and rules so righteous as all this law that I set before you today? (Dt. 4:6–8)

We shouldn't be surprised, therefore, that God requires Moses and the Jews to vanquish the Canaanite nations for their flagrant law-breaking (Dt. 12:1–3); that he commissions Jonah to prophesy against a depraved Nineveh (Jon. 1:1–2); and that, as I noted above, he compels Isaiah to warn and condemn the ancient pagan nations (Is. 15–21). Nor in the New Testament should we find it odd that John the Baptist rebuked Herod for his sexual immorality (Mk. 6:17–18), that Paul and his companions confronted and fought vast numbers of worshippers of the goddess Diana of the Ephesians (Ac. 19), and that Jesus rebuked not simply religious rulers but political rulers as well (Lk. 13:31–32; Jn. 18:34–37). The church, especially her ministers, must occupy a prophetic role in the culture. In an apostate age, the task of Christian leaders is not to accommodate the spirit of the age but to issue to God's people a persistent, clarion call to the authority of the Triune God mediated in the Bible and rebuke the ungodly in society that mock God's gospel and law.

The kingly church

Finally, the church reigns with Jesus Christ in a way appropriate to its earthy state. Paul states this plainly in Ephesians 1:3, 17, 20–23:

> Blessed be the God and Father of our Lord Jesus Christ, who has blessed us in Christ with every spiritual blessing in the heavenly places.... [T]he God of our Lord Jesus Christ, the Father of glory ... raised him from the dead and seated him at his right hand in the heavenly places, far above all rule and authority and power and dominion, and above every name that is named, not only in this age but also in the one to come. And he put all things under his feet and gave him as head over all things to the church, which is his body, the fullness of him who fills all in all.

This means that as Jesus is ruling in the church and over the world, so the church should—and does—share in that reign. This reign isn't triumphalist, and it doesn't exclude trials and hardships (Eph. 6:10–13), but neither do the trials exclude the reign. This reign is the cultural mandate adapted to the post-Fall world. The gospel of Jesus Christ saves sinners, transforming them from rebels to obedient sons and daughters in the Lord's kingdom (Col. 1:12–13), and restoring them to their rightful place as godly deputies in stewarding the earth for his glory. The gospel isn't calculated just to take sinners to heaven, but to fit them for their task of earthly cultural dominion.

The church must fulfill not simply its priestly but also its prophetic and kingly tasks if it's to be faithful to its Lord. This means that *as long as there is sin in the world, there must be a "culture war."*

Conclusion

It's not surprising that many Christians have opted out of the "culture wars." Some have been duped by the political illusion that victories (or defeats) hinge on a single election, and, losing politically, they lose hope and abandon the cultural arena entirely. They don't understand that politics is a short-term manifestation of long-term cultural changes.

Others have (unintentionally) aped the cultural strategies of the political left (media saturation, organizational skills, and educational acumen) and neglected the more vital practices of prayer and Spirit-saturated living. They haven't learned that spiritual victories are won by spiritual resources, though we may employ all legitimate resources God places at our disposal. Or they are simply weary of the battle. There are no battles without casualties, and cultural battles aren't immune to them. Still others, not alert to Christian history and the Christian culture of the West,[13] assume we're living in historically unprecedented times and therefore are convinced we lack the resources for addressing such a massive enemy: the evil is just too great for us. Brian G. Mattson reminds these latter Christians:

> We are not facing unprecedented cultural challenges. It is precisely when people think that this is entirely "new" that ... [w]e think of ourselves as without resources upon which

to draw. And what inevitably happens is fear. Or cynicism. Or despair.

And fear has enough likeness to anger so as to make the caricature of the "angry, bitter Christian" plausible.

There is far too much cultural commentary flowing from the frightened premise: "We're losing our country!" Fear can motivate for a time, but it has no endurance. On the contrary, Christians must be motivated by God's love. Not just in the narrow sense of his redeeming love accomplished and displayed at the cross, but by his love in the broadest sense: loving everything that God loves, including human life and sexual flourishing. And in this we have divinely authorized wisdom from the past, forever encoded for us in the books of the Bible. It continues to speak and shape us, providing a "place to stand," a stabilizing anchor in what appears an unprecedented cultural whirlpool.[14]

We quickly forget that in the antediluvian age, "The Lord saw that the wickedness of man was great in the earth, and that *every* intention of the thoughts of his heart was *only* evil continually" (Gen. 6:5). Every. Only. If there's an example of total cultural depravity, this surely is it. Yet God through a truly unprecedented and never-to-be-repeated judgment overcame that depravity.

Primitive and patristic Christianity emerged and then flourished during the decline and final collapse of the depraved and decadent Roman Empire. During much of this period Rome actively (and sometimes savagely) persecuted Christians. We haven't (yet) been forced to endure this treatment in the West, yet even at that harrowing time God converted Constantine and launched Christendom.

On the eve of the Protestant Reformation the Western church

and culture had become worldly and effete and heretical. From the standpoint of apostasy *within Christendom*, those days seemed unprecedented, yet the Reformation, though imperfect, burst the sinful bonds in church and culture and spurred a great revival whose effects even today haven't totally dissipated.

In each of these eras, the dark days were not the final days, and God sent wholesale revival at what seemed the bleakest time. Similarly, Mattson's point is that in taking "the long view" we can rest in God's good providence and trust that as we're faithful, he'll gradually vanquish his foes, including his cultural foes, in human history. We needn't succumb to feverish fear or to disconsolate despair. Just keep being faithful.

Faithfulness dictates *full-fledged* faithfulness: promoting Jesus-glorifying families, cultivating biblically anchored churches, fostering Christian culture. We don't have the luxury of single-front faithfulness.

In sexually chaotic times, Christians mustn't act in principle differently than they did during more ethically faithful times. We must assume and cultivate and teach—and demand—Christian sexual ethics in family, church and culture. We must recognize God's Word as authoritative in all areas of life and thought. We must rely on God's Spirit to change hearts and lives.

Most importantly: we must at all times worship before the throne of the thrice holy Triune God who is worthy of all glory, laud and honor.

Endnotes to Chapter 5

1   Peter Berger, *The Sacred Canopy* (New York; Anchor, 1967, 1969), 12.

2   Sherif Girgis, Ryan T. Anderson, and Robert P. George, *What is Marriage?* (New York and London: Encounter, 2012), 11.

3   Francis A. Schaeffer, *A Christian Manifesto*, in *The Complete Works of Francis A. Schaeffer* (Westchester, IL: Crossway, 1982), 5:423.

4   Kenneth Minogue, *The Servile Mind* (New York and London: Encounter, 2010), 296.

5   Except one: the state, which exists for the purpose of legally enforcing the "oppression-liberation nexus."

6   Herman Dooyeweerd, *Roots of Western Culture* (Ancaster, ON, Canada: Paideia Press, 2012), 28–36.

7   Dan Scott, "Taking Refuge: Reflections on Same-Sex Marriage," http://christchurchnashville.org/2013/07/01/taking-refuge-reflections-on-same-sex-marriage/. Accessed July 25, 2013.

8   This language was popularized by the late Wheaton College professor Robert Webber, who devoted the last 30 years of his life to prodding evangelicals toward liturgy, the catholic tradition and postmodernism. See his *Ancient-Future Faith* (Grand Rapids: Baker, 1999). It is hard to see how this often accommodationist paradigm contains the resources to combat and overcome our sexually chaotic culture. See Robert H. Gundry, *Jesus the Word According to John the Sectarian* (Grand Rapids: Eerdmans, 2002), 71–94.

9   Brian G. Mattson, "Grace Restores and Perfects Nature: Herman Bavinck and 21st Century Cultural Transformation," http://static.squarespace.com/static/5005c8fe84ae929b3721501f/t/505786a7e4b01fe6ef23c9fe/1347913383382/. Accessed February 15, 2014.

10   John N. Oswalt, *Called to be Holy* (Anderson, IN: Francis Asbury, 1999), 135–147.

11   Herman Ridderbos, *The Coming of the Kingdom* (Phillipsburg, NJ: Presbyterian and Reformed, 1962), 354.

12   Douglas Frank, *Less Than Conquerors* (Eugene, OR: Wipf & Stock, 2009).

13   P. Andrew Sandlin, *Christian Culture* (Mount Hermon, CA: Center for

Cultural Leadership, 2013), 22–28.

14 Brian G. Mattson, "No Country for Old Men: A Modern Parable," http://drbrianmattson.com/journal/2013/7/23/no-country-for-old-men-a-modern-parable. Accessed July 25, 2013.